Contents

Figures   *vi*

Scenarios   *vii*

"What Would You Do?" Cases   *viii*

Introduction   *ix*

1   The Philosophy of Customer Service   *1*
Service as a Traditional Strength in Libraries   *2*
The Spiritual Side of Service   *4*
Organizational Culture and Customer Service   *5*
Responding to a Changing World   *7*

2   Focusing on the Library Customer   *13*
Who Is the Customer?   *14*
Tips from Research on Human Development   *16*
Cultural and Ethnic Differences   *19*
The Role of Life Experiences   *20*

The Library Mission   *21*
The Customer in a Changing Environment   *23*
"The Customer Is Always Right"   *26*
Measuring Customer Satisfaction   *28*

3   What Is Excellence?   *32*
The Complexity of Excellence and Quality   *33*
The Library's Products   *34*
Intangibles and the Augmented Product   *36*
Atmospherics and the Library Environment   *38*
Does a Smile Equal Good Service?   *40*

4   The Team Approach   *44*
Improving Customer Service with Teams   *44*
Forming Teams: Toward an Improved
   Organization   *47*
Administrative Supports   *53*
Integrating Customer Service into Library
   Operations   *55*
Target: Long-Term Relationships—The Development
   of Stakeholders   *57*

5   The Problem-Solving Process   *62*
The Link with Planning   *63*
A Valuable and Necessary Skill   *64*
Reality Check: A Look at Paradigms   *68*
Managing Conflict   *71*
Managing the Emotional Side of Conflict   *73*
The Power of Communication   *75*

**6   Communication: The Language of Customer
Service   *79***
The Phases of Communication   *79*
Active Listening   *82*

CUSTOMER
SERVICE
EXCELLENCE
A Concise Guide for Librarians

DARLENE E. WEINGAND

American Library Association
Chicago and London
1997

While extensive effort has gone into ensuring the reliability of information appearing in this book, the publisher makes no warranty, express or implied, on the accuracy or reliability of the information, and does not assume and hereby disclaims any liability to any person for any loss or damage caused by errors or omissions in this publication.

Project editor: Joan A. Grygel

Cover design: Richmond Jones

Text design: Dianne M. Rooney

Composition: the dotted i on Xyvision using Sabon typeface

Printed on 55-pound Writer's National, a pH-neutral stock, and bound in 10-point C1S cover stock by McNaughton & Gunn, Inc.

The paper used in this publication meets the minimum requirements of American National Standard for Information Sciences—Permanence of Paper for Printed Library Materials, ANSI Z39.48-1992.♾

Library of Congress Cataloging-in-Publication Data
Weingand, Darlene E.
    Customer service excellence : a concise guide for librarians /
  Darlene E. Weingand.
      p.   cm.
    Includes bibliographical references and index.
    ISBN 0-8389-0689-3 (alk. paper)
    1. Libraries and readers—United States. I. Title.
  Z711.W434 1997
  025.5—dc20   96-43394

Printed in the United States of America.

01 00 99 98   5 4 3 2

Nonverbal Communication Messages   *86*
Feedback   *88*
An Intercultural Challenge   *89*
Ten "Magic" Phrases   *91*

7   **Strategies for Success**   *98*
STRATEGY 1: Focus on the Customer   *98*
STRATEGY 2: Enhance Administrative Supports,
   Education, and Training   *100*
STRATEGY 3: Identify Strengths and Limitations   *100*
STRATEGY 4: Set Achievable Goals and
   Objectives   *101*
STRATEGY 5: Commitment: Recognize and
   Acknowledge the Role of Will and Effort   *102*
STRATEGY 6: Keep a Scorecard: How to Tell if
   You're Winning   *103*
STRATEGY 7: Work on Continuous
   Improvement   *106*
STRATEGY 8: Recognize the Power of the
   Customer   *106*
Transforming the Vision   *108*

8   **Looking to the Future through the Lens of
Customer Service**   *113*
Taking a Futurist Perspective   *114*
PRINCIPLE 1   *114*
PRINCIPLE 2   *116*
PRINCIPLE 3   *117*
PRINCIPLE 4   *118*
PRINCIPLE 5   *119*
Achieving and Keeping the Customer Service
   Advantage   *120*

For Further Reading   *125*

Index   *131*

Figures

1.1 The Spiritual Continuum   *4*

2.1 The Library's Customers   *14*

2.2 Hierarchy of Customer Values   *15*

2.3 Hierarchy of Needs   *17*

3.1 The Three-Dimensional Product Mix   *35*

3.2 Product Qualities   *37*

4.1 The Orbit Model   *49*

4.2 The Matrix Model   *50*

5.1 Customer Frustration List   *73*

6.1 Closed and Open-Ended Questions   *80*

6.2 Active Listening Responses   *84*

6.3 The Communication Loop   *88*

6.4 How Culture Influences Us   *92*

7.1 Scorecard for Assessing Progress   *104*

8.1 Customer Service Excellence   *120*

Scenarios

1   The Change Equation   *10*

2   Knowledge about the Library's Customers   *22*

3   A Visit to France   *37*

4   Transforming Teams into Stakeholders   *56*

5   Paradigm Shift in an Academic Library   *70*

6   Two Viewpoints   *90*

7   Putting an Item on Reserve   *107*

8   A Look at Reality   *115*

"What Would You Do?" Cases

1   The Hospital Excuse   *11*

2   The Reference Desk   *30*

3   The Case of the Obsolete Atlas   *42*

4   The Bipolar Team   *60*

5   The Angry Customer   *77*

6   The Challenge of Diversity   *96*

7   The Case of the Cynical City Council   *111*

8   A Study in Alternative Futures   *122*

Introduction

Every author wonders at some point where the idea for a book originates. Sometimes, a colleague poses that question. Since ideas can percolate from the subconscious as well as emerge from an outside stimulus of some kind, it is often difficult to determine the exact source. For this book, however, there are several very clear points of origin.

The first point relates to more of a process than a specific incident. While managing a series of public library branches, I gradually developed a philosophy of customer service that has profoundly influenced how I look at the transaction between library staff and library users. The nature of a public library branch creates an environment that tends to be rather personal in terms of public relations. Many customers are regular users and become very well known to the staff. It is a milieu in which a high standard of customer service can flourish.

The second point of genesis is also a process: the process of teaching and writing about library management for more than fifteen years. Within this process I found a wealth of ideas cross-fertilized through reading, discussing with colleagues and students, and sharing experiences—both positive and negative—with many librarians and library customers from the state of Wisconsin and across the nation.

To this mix I must inevitably add my own reflections on how I have been treated as a library customer in many types of libraries. The issues of time and convenience that are so central to any discussion of customer service affect my life as well. The development of empathy is an attribute that can inform the behavior of any librarian; beginning with one's own needs and preferences is an appropriate and very personal way to begin.

Finally, two very specific catalysts brought all of these ingredients to a "boil." The first occurred during the term of ALA President Hardy Franklin. The presidential theme was, of course, customer service, and many programs were developed that focused on this theme. It was a very effective mechanism for highlighting a critical area of concern to our profession.

The second catalyst occurred last fall during my class "The Public Library." Each student was required to write a term paper. One student selected customer service as a topic and, during the process of seeking bibliographic citations, he was unable to locate many references in the literature of library and information studies. He did, indeed, write the paper—but his citations were drawn primarily from business and management literature.

The sum of these occurrences has led to this book. When a concept that is so essential to successful professional practice is fundamentally absent from that profession's literature, a clear mandate emerges to contribute to filling that void. This book is one author's attempt to make that contribution. The title reflects the twin themes of customer service as both a mandate and the goal of service excellence.

Organization

Customer Service Excellence is divided into eight chapters. The first chapter introduces the philosophy of service from an overall perspective and then, more specifically, with regard to libraries. Service is one of the cornerstones of the library's product and must, therefore, assume the role of foundation for the chapters to follow.

Chapter two focuses on the library customer. Who is the customer? (The answer to this question may surprise you!) A brief excursion into human development research helps to provide some depth to the discussion; cultural and ethnic differences are presented as part of the equation. This convergence of developmental theory and diversity identifies each customer as a multifaceted individual having unique and very special needs. It is a challenge, an opportunity, and a delight to identify the customer's needs and bring together the appropriate resources to respond to those needs.

In chapter three the topic addressed is "excellence," particularly in terms of quality. The library's product becomes the centerpiece to this discussion, and considerable attention is given to the multiple aspects of "product." How excellence and product interact within the overall operations of the library is key to customer satisfaction—and, thereby, central to customer service.

The team approach to developing a successful customer service approach is covered in chapter four. The formation of teams and possible structures for teams are one of the effective mechanisms for integrating customer service into library operations. With the ultimate target of developing "stakeholder" involvement in the library and the community it serves, these teams are charged with the improvement of both visible and invisible services.

Problem solving is the subject of chapter five. Presented as a valuable and necessary skill in this century and into the next, problem solving is essential to managing conflicts and the emotional side of conflict. Communication is a core component of problem solving, and the art of listening is presented as integral to effective communication.

Customer service also has a "language." Expanding on the previous discussion of problem solving, chapter six looks at verbal and nonverbal communication messages with an emphasis on the feedback loop. Special "magic" phrases that can facilitate the customer service effort are presented; while not truly "magic," these phrases can smooth the process and move the library closer to its goal.

Chapter seven summarizes what has gone before by identifying strategies for success. There are many facets to such a jewel, including identifying strengths and limitations and setting achievable goals and objectives. Education and training of staff must be integrated into the entire effort; administrative and staff commitment is presented as the glue that holds it all together.

Finally, chapter eight looks toward the future and focuses on the futurist perspective in developing excellent customer service. Five principles are presented, culminating in a discussion of achieving and keeping the customer service advantage.

The "What would you do?" sections in each chapter pose customer service dilemmas along with possible responses.

Excellent customer service is more than a goal . . . more than an ideal . . . and more than the jargon of the '90s. It is, in its most basic form, good business practice. Whether a business is for-profit or nonprofit, with products that are tangible or intangible, customer service is the axis around which all other operations must revolve. *Customer Service Excellence* seeks to strengthen the campaign so enthusiastically inaugurated in Hardy Franklin's presidential year. It is customer service that must drive the libraries of the twenty-first century; it is customer service that will be a key factor in whether a library survives— or thrives—in the new millennium.

1

The Philosophy of Customer Service

What is service?

> work done or duty performed for another or others
> respect; attention; devotion
> helpful, beneficial, or friendly action or conduct
> act giving assistance or advantage to another
> activity carried on to provide people with the use of something
> the quality of that which is provided[1]

These dictionary definitions are part of a long series of definitions; they range from the work itself to how the work is provided and finally to the quality of the work. This is quite a range, but it also illustrates the complexity of the service concept.

Service as a Traditional Strength in Libraries

"Libraries are service organizations." This is a statement that most librarians believe in and would ratify. Yet, if it were true all the time in every library, there would be little or no need for this book.

Service has been viewed for many years as one of the library's strengths. As with all generalizations, such a statement applies in greater or lesser degree to any specific library. However, generalizations are also usually based on at least a kernel of fact, and many library staff members work long hours with the *intent* of providing good service. Yet, while many people decide to seek positions in libraries because of a genuine desire to be helpful and to work with people, others find library employment appealing because they envision working *with books* in a solitary or isolated way. The service ethic is, indeed, a historical and traditional foundation of library operations, but it ebbs and flows from library to library.

However, even in those libraries in which the service ethos is strong, there are library staff who, while claiming to believe in service, shy away from using the word *customer* or even thinking of people who use libraries as "customers." More commonly, the preferred word is *patron* and, occasionally, *user.* Since language is a reflection of thought, these terms are quite telling. The word *patron* is associated with the act of giving support and protection, such as occurred in the Renaissance between royalty and artists. The impression here is one of unequal status, of the more powerful protecting the less powerful. This is not the type of relationship that puts libraries on an equal level of partnership with their communities. Further, while *user* accurately describes someone who uses the library, the term is quite unspecific and is widely associated with the drug culture.

The word *customer,* which implies payment for a product or service, is a better reflection of what actually transpires between the library and people in the community. With this term the mythology of the "free" library is dispelled, and a more accurate metaphor for service is substituted.

Lillian N. Gerhardt, editor-in-chief of *School Library Journal,* in reflecting on Hardy Franklin's selection of customer service as the theme of his ALA presidential year, said that, "'Customer' suits children and young adults in libraries far better than 'patron,' 'client,' or 'user' ever did. Best of all, it raises them to a level of equality with adult customers as the other common terms never quite managed to do."[2] If libraries are to transform the service tradition from a vague philosophy into a vital operational mandate, the perception and use of the term *library customer* is a good first step.

Another lens through which to view the use of language is the *paradigm*. A paradigm is a pattern or model that exerts considerable influence over how people think and behave. Librarians who flinch at the word *customer* are operating out of an outmoded paradigm. This older paradigm portrays the library as a "public good," with as high a ranking on the "goodness" scale as the national flag, parenthood, and apple pie. As a public good, the library "should" receive public support. However, today's library is in increasingly tight competition for declining resources, and unless it adopts and masters the language and techniques of its competitors, it faces a future of declining support and significance.

This does not imply that all librarians operate out of the old paradigm. Hardy Franklin views every community member as a customer and states that this "is an apt way to remind ourselves—and our staffs—of the manner in which we wish to associate with the public."[3] This is a mind shift of major proportions. If every community member, library user or not, is perceived as a present or potential customer—free to give his or her information business to the library or to any other information source—then we've taken a major step toward operating under a new paradigm.

Perhaps a more accurate view of libraries as service organizations would include the marketing perspective that libraries have service as a component of their product mix. The actual work done in a library is a part of service and analogous to the concept of "core product" that is presented in chapter 3. This is the mechanical aspect of service without which no actual service is performed.

However, though it is essential to the customer service function, actual work is insufficient without the philosophy or spirit that enriches and enlivens it. Karl Albrecht, author of *The Only*

Thing That Matters: Bringing the Power of the Customer into the Center of Your Business, states that, "Many organizations will fail in their quest for total quality service, not because their leaders don't understand the conceptual or technical requirements for achieving it, but because they don't realize that the heart of the service journey is spiritual rather than mechanical."[4] This spiritual aspect of service is the true motivator and, when present, animates customer service.

The Spiritual Side of Service

The spirit of service may be unseen, but it moves organizations and people to perform. Albrecht characterizes the *spirit of service* as "an attitude based on certain values and beliefs about people, life, and work, that leads a person to willingly serve others and take pride in his or her work."[5]

Values, attitudes, and beliefs mold the way employees perceive themselves, their customers, and their work. Each organization has a dominant orientation that creates and defines the company's culture; this orientation may be either technological, rational, or financial. It is the elements of this orientation that are seen as important and govern "the way we do things around here."[6]

Every organization has a spiritual essence; libraries are no exception. This spirit can be placed on a continuum from negative to positive (see figure 1.1). At the extreme negative end, the library suffers from poor staff morale that inevitably carries over into poor customer service. At the opposite pole of the continuum, positive organizational climate results in high staff morale and the customers benefit.

Figure 1.1   The Spiritual Continuum

(–)		(+)
Negative environment; poor morale		Positive environment; high morale

Organizational Culture and Customer Service

Organizational culture has such a profound effect on staff morale and interaction with customers that service quality must be examined through the organizational perspective. Librarians with even the best service orientation will find it problematic to provide a high level of service if the operating environment does not encourage and empower the staff to provide this level of service. Conversely, library staff with less enthusiasm for customer service to begin with may be energized when management encourages and rewards a positive service attitude.

As an illustration of how an organizational climate can positively influence customer service, Robert J. Rauscher, vice president of marketing at Amoco Oil, has stated that, "The only way to provide consistent customer service is to have each employee focus attention on how he/she impacts the ultimate customer—and identify ways to consistently exceed customer expectations."[7] However, *employees cannot create this focus without the support of the organizational culture.* While the beginnings of consistent customer service may bubble up from anywhere in the organization, a sustaining wellspring of management support is necessary to ensure its continuity.

Dynamic System Theory suggests that people are not victims of their environment but, rather, have the ability to create and control circumstances. Such a system is composed of input, feedback, and reality.[8] In communication terms, *input* consists of the suggestions and ideas that customers and staff provide—or do not provide. *Feedback* completes the communication loop and channels back to the initial communicator some kind of result or reaction, whether the suggestion is accepted or rejected—and why. *Reality* is the set of environmental conditions and restraints that mediate communication outcomes.

What factors produce the organizational environment of the library? Here, too, the elements of input, feedback, and reality frame the environment. The library operating within a negative framework may have

input of poor customer focus or commitment

strategies that serve the organization rather than customers a lack of awareness of customer needs

inadequate (or no) process of performance measurement

little problem-solving action

deficient training or empowerment of staff members

In this case, consequent outcomes (or feedback) could include

poor public image and publicity

unsatisfied customers

high costs in terms of productivity and staff time

pressure on staff to do more with less

high staff turnover and low morale

a decline in market share

The final piece—reality—is actually present in two very different parts: the way library staff members see things, with customer satisfaction as a likely afterthought, and what really is, with customers having the power to choose where their business will be directed.[9]

Moving toward a positive framework for service, possible inputs might include

a library management that is committed to and focused on customers

an identification of customer needs with appropriate responses

formal performance measurements

customer-friendly policies and strategies

trained and empowered staff at all levels

an ongoing goal of continuous improvement that is both recognized and rewarded

When these inputs are in place, feedback can take various forms:

a positive library image

loyal customers

increased funding and support

more cost-effective operations

motivated and empowered library staff

increased market share

The two-part reality occurs in the library's commitment to customer service and success and growth—in thriving, not just surviving.[10]

The exciting part of this dynamic system model is the *control* that rests in the hands of library management and staff. Leadership is not a quality that is confined to positions of authority. Rather, leadership may flourish at all staff levels. Since customers form their perceptions of an organization from those staff members *with whom they interact,* the belief and behavioral systems that are operative throughout the library ultimately affect the way customers act and react. When employee leadership is fostered and encouraged, the ripple effect will extend beyond the staff to the library's customers.

Even in a library that does not have a tradition of staff empowerment, management attitudes can change. When change is introduced to any aspect of operations, the other components also shift. Thus, it is possible to have direct and far-reaching influence on the entire system. Service to customers grows out of and reinforces service to *employees,* which ultimately benefits the total library organization—a cycle of growth and quality that continually reinvents itself.

Responding to a Changing World

Too often, organizational culture is rooted in tradition and habit, and change is often an unwelcome visitor. Yet, change is today's one constant, and no organization can escape its presence and its effects. Whether regarded as an opportunity or as a threat, the specter of change sits on every organization's board of directors; the library is no exception.

Lucier and Dooley, in their article, "Cosmology and the Changing Role of Libraries," argue that, "Library administrators have the responsibility to create organizational climates that encourage and promote change. . . . The great responsibility, however, rests with the individual who must adapt and adopt the idea of continual change as a goal and a mode of both personal and organizational operation."[11] Indeed, it is the individual employee upon whose shoulders the burden and challenge of change inevitably rest.

As change percolates throughout the information field, libraries must redefine their missions, goals and objectives, planning and marketing processes—in other words, the way they do business. Libraries that cling to traditional models of operation or elect to maintain the status quo will proceed slowly and laboriously into the next century, relating less and less to their customers and ultimately losing the support needed to continue operations. These are the libraries that hold fast to a view of library service that still connects to yesterday's paradigms. The library's management has lost sight of the many changes in customer needs and expectations. To survive, an organization must adapt; if it does not adapt, it cannot ensure—or assume— survival.

However, those who think and write about the future do not believe in a world of predestination—even technological predestination. Rather, prevailing wisdom recommends a proactive stance that determines a preferred future and works vigorously toward its realization. The result of inaction is that the future will occur on its own, but it may not be the one that is desired. The future of libraries *can* be shaped, and it must be people— not technology—that shape them.

How does this discussion of change relate to the philosophy of service? Or:

> How can the library create and maintain *excellence* in a *changing environment* where responding to *customer needs* and focusing on *customer satisfaction* determines *survival* and *prosperity*?

This question contains key words and phrases that appear in italicized type and are all the essential elements of customer service: *Excellence (E), Changing Environment (CE), Customer Needs (CN), Customer Service (CS), Survival (S),* and *Prosperity (P).* For the mathematically inclined, here's an equation:

$$\frac{E \times X^{CE}}{CN + CS} = S + P$$

As with all equations, the two sides must balance. Therefore, to obtain the sum of survival and prosperity, a library must multiply excellent products and service by the unknown quantity of a changing environment and divide that product by the needs and expectations of customers. If any of the elements of this equation are not present, the two sides will not balance. Scenario 1 shows the differences in customer service in libraries that heed the traditional paradigm and libraries that focus on the customer.

In a closer examination of the parts of this equation, customer needs and expectations will be the focus of chapter 2, and excellence will be addressed in detail in chapter 3.

Regarding the unknown variable, the "X factor" or changing environment, professor of library and information studies Michael Buckland argues that, "Any change in technology that would have a significant effect on the methods available for acquisition, storage, delivery, or searching procedures could have important consequences for library service. Consequently, a continuing quest for technological improvement has been and should continue to be important."[12] The nature of such a quest leads inevitably to an ongoing, changing environment, some of which we may anticipate but that also includes unpredictable elements.

Buckland further asserts that, "As operations and services become more complex and more capital-intensive, ad hoc, unsystematic decision making can lead library services down unproductive paths. Correcting mistakes becomes expensive and disruptive. Creative planning is of central importance because of the superiority of planning over merely reacting to events."[13] This endorsement of *planning* as a management tool, critical in a changing environment, cannot receive too much emphasis. Going a step further, however, unless planning takes place *with the customer as the pivot point,* it cannot carry the library forward vigorously into the new century.

Customer service excellence begins with a restless dissatisfaction with the status quo and the belief that one can do better.[14] It is the variable in the equation that is truly attainable, given adequate determination and effort. It is a challenge that is always present and a reward that is well worth pursuing.

SCENARIO 1

The Change Equation

Factor	Worst Case	Best Case
Excellence	Customers often hear: "We don't have it" . . . period.	Customers always hear: "That item is not available today, but we can get it for you."
Changing Environment	School and academic libraries in town have Internet capability, but the public library does not.	The library is actively involved in the local freenet and also offers Internet access on site.
Customer Needs	A local company works three shifts; therefore, many customers cannot come to the library when it is open.	The customers who work at that company know that the library will respond to their needs. (See Customer Service, following.)
Customer Service	The staff favors staff convenience over customer convenience. Staff are often abrupt and appear to be overly busy.	The library offers a dial-in public access catalog that also allows customers to request reserves and interlibrary loans. Materials are delivered to special locations in town where customers can retrieve them during convenient hours. Information is transmitted to customers by E-mail.
Survival	Many customers now use the services of the library in the neighboring town.	The library is enthusiastically regarded by the community.
Prosperity	The library receives declining support from the community.	A new building is overwhelmingly approved. Citizens regard serving on the library board as an honor.

■ 1 ■

The Hospital Excuse

Peter is staffing the circulation desk when a woman approaches. She looks tired and somewhat pale—and quite ill at ease. She puts a stack of books and videos on the desk and, in a somewhat embarrassed voice, states that the materials are three weeks overdue. Peter looks through the materials and determines that the total fines due would be $30. The customer apologizes for the overdue materials and explains that she has recently been released from the hospital. She adds that she realizes that library policy will keep her from checking out more materials until the fine is paid—but with hospital bills to pay, she cannot pay the fines at this time.

Meanwhile, several customers have come into the library and are waiting to return their materials. They can easily hear the conversation between Peter and the first customer.

How could Peter proceed?

One Possible Response

Although Peter has the responsibility for implementing library policies, he also has been given discretionary judgment by the director. He assures the customer that he understands why the materials are late and apologizes for any worry that may have added to her health and economic problems. He tells her that the accrued fines will not be assessed and wishes her a speedy recovery. In addition, he asks whether she needs assistance in locating materials to check out for her convalescent period.

Questions to Consider

- Are library policies designed to be bent or broken? Under what circumstances?
- Should Peter have consulted the library director?
- Several customers witnessed this encounter. Should Peter explain the extraordinary circumstances to these customers?
- How much discretion should be given to circulation staff?
- Some customers may use excuses to avoid following library policies. How can the library determine the difference between a legitimate excuse and an attempt to take advantage?

Is there a better way to handle this situation? You decide.

Notes

1. *Webster's New Twentieth Century Dictionary of the English Language,* unabridged 2d ed. (William Collins + World, 1975), 1,658.

2. Lillian N. Gerhardt, "'Customers' Just the Right Word," *School Library Journal* 40, no. 6 (June 1994): 4.

3. Hardy G. Franklin, "Customer Service: The Heart of a Library," *College & Research Libraries News* 2 (Feb. 1994): 63.

4. Karl Albrecht, *The Only Thing That Matters: Bringing the Power of the Customer into the Center of Your Business* (New York: Harper, 1992), 87.

5. Albrecht, 88.

6. Albrecht, 87.

7. Robert J. Rauscher, as quoted in Robert L. Desatnick and Denis H. Detzel, *Managing to Keep the Customer: How to Achieve and Maintain Superior Customer Service throughout the Organization,* rev. ed. (San Francisco: Jossey-Bass, 1993), 65.

8. The work of Ludwig von Bertalanffy, as presented in Joan Koob Cannie with Donald Kaplin, *Keeping Customers for Life* (New York: American Management Assn., 1991), 19.

9. Adapted from Cannie, 19.

10. Adapted from Cannie, 19–20.

11. R. E. Lucier and J. F. Dooley, "Cosmology and the Changing Role of Libraries: An Analogy and Reflections," *Journal of the American Society for Information Science* 36, no. 1 (Jan. 1985): 47.

12. Michael Buckland, *Redesigning Library Services: A Manifesto* (Chicago: ALA, 1992), 1.

13. Buckland, 8.

14. Desatnick and Detzel, 18.

2

❧

Focusing on the Library Customer

Library operations don't occur in a vacuum. They take place within an institutional culture and environment. This institutional milieu creates the service atmosphere and significantly influences the approach that staff members take when performing routine tasks. In libraries where a commitment to service is present but at a minimum level, the institutional culture may be task oriented; administrative and staff concerns are directed toward the successful, efficient completion of routine duties.

At the opposite end of the continuum the library culture regards customer satisfaction as the primary goal, and both administrators and staff direct their energies and activities toward that goal. Naturally, there are many points on the continuum between these two attitudinal poles; the key concept is one of the library's mission-driving functions.

The central message of this chapter is to underscore the importance of positioning the library close to the customer-oriented end of the continuum together with a discussion of customer identity, needs, and interests. This usually requires a change in mindset among those in the organization.

Who Is the Customer?

It would be the rare library employee who would not be able to give an answer to this question. However, the response would typically be "the patron, the person who uses the library." This is, of course, an accurate statement—but one that only partially addresses the question and that lingers inside the old paradigm (recognized by the use of the term *patron*). Because library employees believe the statement to be true, that belief becomes the primary obstacle to understanding customers.

If the library user can be characterized as a customer, what other customers can be identified? Marketing theory portrays customers as both external and internal and arranges them as potential target markets. Carrying this approach forward into the library environment, figure 2.1 illustrates how library customers might be categorized.

Figure 2.1 The Library's Customers

Internal	*External*
Administration	Library users
Employees	Library nonusers
Funding authorities/policymakers	Vendors
Volunteers and others	Funders
	Legislators and others

Simply limiting the definition of customer to library users severely restricts any opportunity to develop a comprehensive customer service policy. A more productive approach to identifying customers in a specific library can emerge from the appointment of a planning team that collectively determines the full range of customers unique to that library's environment. The team's composition should also reflect the diverse target markets served by the library.

As noted earlier, what one already believes can stand in the way of learning and changing behavior. The longer an employee works in the library, the stronger the belief becomes—resulting in a weakened opportunity to understand customer needs and preferences. This is where the planning team can be particularly useful. When the members of the team represent various constituency groups, they bring a broader perspective concerning the identity and preferences of various customers.

Albrecht looks at customer research in a nonmeasurement context: through the customer's perception of value (see figure 2.2). He adapts Abraham Maslow's hierarchy of human needs (see figure 2.3) to create a hierarchy of customer value.

Figure 2.2   Hierarchy of Customer Values

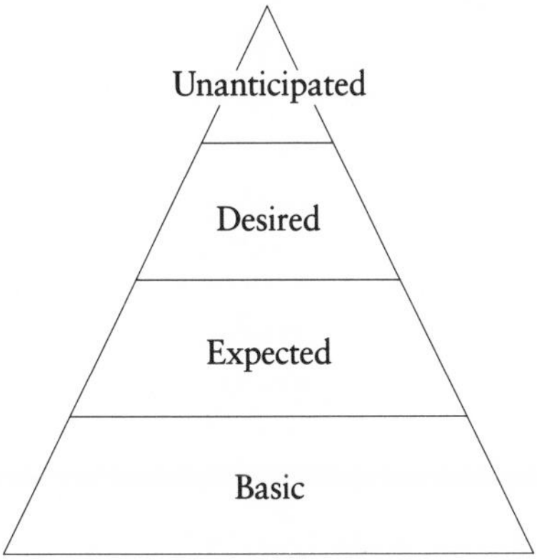

Unanticipated: Beyond the known

Desired: Not expected, but known and appreciated

Expected: Attributes that the customer takes for granted

Basic: The essential attributes of the experience

Source: Karl Albrecht, *The Only Thing That Matters: Bringing the Power of the Customer into the Center of Your Business* (New York: Harper, 1992), 112–14.

Using the library environment, note the following levels of these values.

Basic: A building containing print and audiovisual materials

Expected: Competent assistance of staff in finding information and materials; clean, attractive surroundings

Desired: Needed materials secured through interlibrary loan from another library; cheerful, helpful, and pleasant staff attitudes

Unanticipated: Referral to another person or agency; information available through computer linkups

The perceived value is the key to understanding customers' satisfaction and how they view the benefit from each level. Focusing on the customer in this way clarifies the relationship between library operations and benefits to the consumer. Clearly, the size and completeness of the library's collection relates mostly to the basic level. However, this aspect of library operations usually consumes a large portion of staff time and energy. To connect more directly with customer satisfaction, the higher levels of value must be actively addressed.

The use of customer focus groups can provide considerable insight into the values that are operative in specific library situations. Focus groups are made up of invited participants who share some common attributes. A trained facilitator leads the members of the group through a series of questions designed to encourage discussion. The questions begin with general issues regarding the library and proceed into increasingly more-specific concepts. Through focus groups, you can distinguish library customer expectations.

Tips from Research on Human Development

Unfortunately, sometimes a staff attitude emerges that views the customer as a faceless, homogeneous entity rather than as a collection of individuals. It is important to impress on library staff that all customers are driven by motives similar to their own: a wish to succeed in their jobs, a wish for security for their families and themselves, a desire for recognition, and safety and self-preservation.[1] Author Russell Robinson, in his discussion of adult motivation, interpreted psychologist Abraham Maslow's hierarchy of needs, in which he arranged five levels of needs within a triangular framework, as shown in figure 2.3. These needs are a constant throughout life and are representative of what it means to be a human being. They build upon each other in a hierarchical fashion. In other words, if a level of need is only partially met, one's energies remain at that level until those needs are satisfied. For example, if someone is seriously hungry, it is unrealistic to expect that person to be concerned about safety or social activities.

Figure 2.3 Hierarchy of Needs

Self-actualization: A sense of accomplishment and the development and utilization of one's potential

Self-esteem needs: Those which reflect on an individual's self-worth and self-confidence

Social needs: A sense of belonging and acceptance by others

Security needs: A projection of physiological needs into the future, including protection from physical harm, assurance of continuing income and employment, etc.

Physiological needs: The most-basic needs necessary to sustain survival, such as food, air, and sleep

SOURCE: Russell D. Robinson, *An Introduction to Helping Adults Learn and Change* (Milwaukee, Wisc.: Omnibook, 1979), 10.

How does this example relate to library service and to a focus on the customer? In a scenario in which a customer enters the library in search of information on a local food bank, the appropriate library response should be immediate referral to a local source of complimentary or low-cost food or meals—and not an armful of cookbooks! While this may seem to be a fanciful example, it is not. Too often, library staff operate out of a mindset that is rooted in available library materials rather than in a perspective of providing information in the broadest sense.

Beyond those attributes that cover the life span, other attributes—organized in stages—are also shared by all people. A number of well-respected theorists have proposed stage theories, including Gould, Levinson, Vaillant, Erikson, and Neugarten.[2] The concept of stages was popularized by Sheehy in the best-selling book *Passages: Predictable Crises of Adult Life* and recently updated in *New Passages: Mapping Your Life Across Time* to more closely relate to today's society.[3] The following synthesis of the adult years illustrates the overall pattern of thought behind stage theory.

Age 18–22   Leaving the family and establishing life on one's own; may include getting an additional education, beginning work, establishing a separate home, developing peer relationships, and managing time and money

Age 22–28   Becoming independent; setting the patterns of life in motion; finding a mentor; entering the world of work; selecting a mate; having a feeling of invincibility; feeling confident and optimistic

Age 28–33   The "age 30" transition; questioning of earlier choices; having feelings of doubt and dissatisfaction and desiring change; a contradictory time of wanting to broaden and extend oneself and to find stability and roots; may involve changing jobs, buying a house, having a baby, getting a divorce

Age 33–38   Putting down roots and extending; becoming one's own person; developing competence and establishing one's niche in society; working at career success; a time of conflicting time demands

Age 38–46   Midlife transition (middle-age crisis); having a feeling that time is running out; a time of dissatisfaction and reexamination of life and priorities; often an unstable time resembling adolescence; reassessing personal relationships and career goals; searching for meaning

Age 46–53   Restabilization and self-acceptance; a time of mellowing and settling down; developing a new life structure; discovering that one is ultimately alone

Age 53–60   A time of either renewal or resignation; maintaining position or changing roles; a time of increased personal happiness and satisfaction; developing hobbies and secondary interests in preparation for later years

Age 60–65   Late adulthood transition and anticipation or fear of retirement; a difficult time for those who have defined themselves by their careers; confronting loss (of job, home, spouse); adjusting to less income; preparing for the years to come

Age 65+   Late adulthood; having a feeling of fulfillment or failure; searching for the meaning of one's life[4]

These stages are approximate, and while people pass through them in a sequential manner, the exact ages will vary from individual to individual. Indeed, Sheehy maintains that even these approximations have shifted and are no longer normative. She claims that there is a revolution in the life cycle, and within a single generation, the shape of the life cycle has been fundamentally altered. To illustrate, she offers the following observations:

People are leaving childhood at a younger age.

Puberty arrives earlier.

Adolescence is now prolonged (for the middle class) until the end of the twenties.

More young adults live at home longer.

True adulthood doesn't begin until thirty.

Feeling fully "grown up" may not happen until the forties.

Middle age has been pushed far into the fifties.

Most middle-aged Americans still have a living parent.

People are taking longer to die.[5]

These observations suggest that the entire life cycle has shifted forward about a decade, with corresponding movement in each of the stages occurring in later years. In attempting to understand the library customer, consider not only the life stages but also the marker events that might have moved in response to changing conditions.

Cultural and Ethnic Differences

Individual human-development characteristics are, however, fundamentally influenced by cultural, ethnic, and racial attributes.

As a person matures through life, these three sets of attributes profoundly define who that person is, how the world is viewed, what expectations are held, when certain milestones take place, where he or she fits into society, and why life is worth living. For example, a woman who grows up in an urban ghetto environment may believe that she is limited by poverty and view the world as fundamentally hostile. She may see her future in relation to the children she brings into the world and feel that her racial or ethnic environment is the only part of society that will accept her. She may view life as something to survive rather than to enjoy. This woman may think that power is externally imposed rather than internal and under her control. Another woman who is born into a positive environment may have a sense of empowerment and hope. She may see the world as a challenge, but one that can be met. She may believe in herself and seek out the education and experiences that will enable her to succeed. She may feel that she is self-empowered and that her life is under her control. She may view life as a series of opportunities that will enrich her.

In other words, a person's philosophical and spiritual outlook is molded and shaped by the environment into which he or she is born as well as by the developmental factors that are common to humankind. Too often, attempts to define the customer are limited by perceptions focusing on a facet of the individual rather than the entire three-dimensional human being. Even when we recognize human-development characteristics, forgetting about the profound effects of culture, ethnicity, and race upon the individual's environment seriously compromises our full understanding. If anything, library customers are a very diverse group.

The Role of Life Experiences

In addition to human development characteristics and cultural/ethnic/racial attributes, each customer also possesses a lifetime of experiences from which a variety of interests and inclinations have emerged. It's not always possible to determine life experiences from simply meeting customers. However, from the customer focus groups suggested earlier, it's possible to determine the following value elements of a library that typically drive customers' preferences and perceptions:

Environmental values: The physical setting in which the customer and the product are brought together in a library building, over a telephone line, or through a computer connection.

Aesthetic values: The sensory experience that the customer encounters, including visual elements, sounds, color, heat, light, physical arrangement of objects, and psychological factors.

Interpersonal values: Interactions between the customer and staff, and between the individual and other customers; includes the presence or absence of courtesy, friendliness, helpfulness, and competence.

Procedural values: The factors in a transaction, including time spent waiting and explaining, the need to fill out forms, considerations such as circulation limits and policies, hours of operation, and the relative convenience of the procedures.

Informational values: The customer's experience in gaining information through questions, signage, and policies and procedures.

Deliverable values: The physical products that are given to the customer, such as books and other materials, computer printouts, and referrals.

Financial values: The cost to the customer for the total experience, including taxes, fees, or fines.[6]

Scenario 2 identifies what happens to customer service when staff are knowledgeable about their customers.

The Library Mission

The sum of the values uncovered from a customer focus group should become central to the development of the library's service strategy—the part of the planning process that evolves within and as a result of the library's mission. Librarians have

SCENARIO 2

Knowledge about the Library's Customers

Customer Attributes	Worst Case	Best Case
Internal Customers	Staff are not regarded as customers.	Staff needs are identified and responded to as soon as possible.
External Customers	Only customers who use the library are considered. They are viewed simplistically as "library users."	Community analysis is done regularly. Target markets are identified. Selective dissemination of information (SDI), that is, information on customer interests and needs is gathered and relevant materials are delivered to customers before they need to ask, is a regular library service.
Maslow's Needs Developmental Needs	No consideration is given to staff or customer needs.	Staff are trained and knowledgeable. Customers are considered in terms of their possible levels of need.
Cultural/Ethnic Differences	No consideration is given.	Staff are trained and knowledgeable. Cultural differences are always considered.
Life Experience	No consideration is given.	Staff are aware of the importance of acquired experience in adult learning and build upon it when determining appropriate information and materials.

often underrated the mission in its importance to the planning process. Rather than being a simple paragraph of scope, audience, and intent, the mission must also incorporate a statement of service philosophy that can evolve naturally into library practice. In many ways, developing a mission statement may take more time and involve more discussion than any of the more pragmatic steps that follow. Certainly, the importance of the library's mission cannot be emphasized too strongly, and sufficient time must be allocated to its shared development.

Unfortunately, many mission statements are primarily internally focused on staff goals and products: what the library will and will not do, and what it will and will not provide. However, the mission statement that will move a library vigorously and successfully into the next century will shift that focus from internal operations to an external service strategy—with customer interests and preferences as the driving force.

The Customer in a Changing Environment

In developing the library's service strategy, consider the values discussed in the previous section in the context of today's rapidly changing environment. If you clearly define a group of target customers and if you understand their service expectations, then the design of the service strategy is greatly simplified.[7]

In considering such a design, Buckland states that two relationships become important in providing library services:

> How will changes in the provision of library services affect library users and what they do?

> How should changes in the tasks and work habits of library users affect the provision of library services?[8]

Provision of Library Services

Automation has fundamentally altered the library's internal environment. Many of these "backstage" developments have not been visible to the library's customers. However, once automation was applied to the library's catalog, customers became aware not only of a physical change but also of a significant improvement in access. For customers of some libraries, the route to access has extended beyond the library's walls to the home or work computer via telephone lines.

Not only has the linkage between customer and library been enhanced but the information and materials available to customers have also multiplied as libraries extend their reach electronically to increasing numbers of databases, bibliographic records, and interlibrary loans. However, it's important to remember that these nonpersonal contacts will also determine customers' experiences and, ultimately, their satisfaction.

Customer Work Habits

How will this electronic revolution influence customer work habits and, ultimately, customer expectations? Since the revolution has become pervasive in the culture, communicating electronically has become part of the operational environment of many of the library's customers. Routine use of computers, electronic mail, the Internet, and the World Wide Web has connected the workplace to a global infrastructure. Libraries have become a key part of this infrastructure, and the interaction between present and potential library customers will rest in large part upon a redefinition of customer service in the electronic age.

Such a redefinition can best be accomplished if it is approached from the customer's point of view rather than from the perspective of the library's internal operations. In "prerevolutionary" times, a customer service policy would have considered customer preferences in terms of such factors as

hours of operation

size and content of the collection

building ambiance: signage, furniture, color, heat, and light

parking

staff attitude

library programs

In the present "postrevolutionary" period, while these factors are still present and important to many customers, additional ones include access to catalog from work or home

placing holds on materials from work or home

speedy delivery systems

remote access to databases, CD-ROM products, etc.

facsimile transmission of documents

instruction in the use of library sources

referrals to other sources or providers

If a library is going to survive—and thrive—in this new electronic environment, it will have to let the market (its customers) define value. Although the library's products and services may conform perfectly to internal specifications or standards of quality, if they do not meet market requirements, they will not succeed with customers.

Today, market requirements are being influenced by ever-rising expectations of service—an economic, social, and political phenomenon. Overall, consumers have more income and are better educated than ever before; therefore, they are more demanding about the service they receive. Not only are service expectations higher today but they will continue to grow because customers are becoming more sophisticated and less willing to believe that a product, by itself without service and support, can do the job.[9]

Therefore, it is essential to determine what the library customer wants. In a recent survey considering manufactured items, the most important items were, in rank order, performance, durability, ease of repair, service availability, warranty, and ease of use. Out of nine factors, price was ranked a distant seventh; appearance and brand name received the lowest ratings.[10]

The same survey also defined service quality: courtesy, promptness, a sense that one's needs were being satisfied, and a good service-provider attitude. Factors such as accuracy, convenience, and trouble-free service were less frequently mentioned. We can conclude that a customer's perception of being treated with care and respect can minimize other service difficulties.[11]

What implications does this survey have for libraries? Looking at specific "frontrunners" of market desires as reported by the survey, we can draw the following implications for the library:

Performance: Condition of library materials, appropriateness of materials and information, speed of delivery, and ease of access (in many ways, an overarching term covering the rest of the factors)

Durability: Condition of materials and quality of information

Ease of repair: Interaction with library staff concerning inappropriate materials or information and search for "replacements"

Service availability: Access to library services, whether that be through hours of operation or computer linkage

Warranty: Staff assurance that if the customer is not satisfied, recontact should be made

Ease of use: Good signage within buildings, user-friendly catalog and computer access, convenient delivery systems

Courtesy: Staff attitude and interaction

Promptness: Timely delivery of materials, response to questions, and telephone and computer interactions

Satisfaction of needs: Belief that questions were answered satisfactorily and appropriate materials were procured in a timely and convenient way

Trouble-free service: Helpful, cheerful staff and a remedy of any difficulties

Moreover, as previously noted, when the customer is treated with care and respect, many shortcomings in any of these areas can be significantly alleviated. While the translation from the manufacturing world to nonprofit library service may be stretched in places, overall the concepts are readily transferable.

"The Customer Is Always Right"

The quotation in the heading has been attributed to Marshall Field, and it has a long history within the retail trade. The sentiment underlying the quote has evolved through the years to be the genesis of the focus on customer satisfaction. If, indeed, the customer is always right, then all services and operations would be designed to meet, or exceed, customer expectations. This service attitude has been extremely successful for the retail trade and, when applied to the nonprofit sector, produces similar positive results.

In addition to identifying who the customer is and what she or he wants and expects, there is another critical and essential component that makes it all work—or not work: carefully selected and trained and justly rewarded contact personnel. Living up to the philosophy that the customer is always right can produce significant strain on library employees. Work at the "boundary" between customers and the library creates stress for service workers because they must simultaneously satisfy both the organization and its customers.[12] Every potential and present employee is not automatically suited by personality or temperament to work at this boundary. In determining which staff members are to be placed in personal-contact jobs, four criteria should be applied. Employees must be both motivated and able to

1. deliver service that meets customer expectations
2. recover when there has been a service failure, display behaviors beyond customer expectations, and satisfy expectations regarding special requests
3. behave in ways that make customers feel secure and justly treated
4. act as supervisors of and colleagues with (internal) customers who are involved in coproducing the service[13]

Unfortunately, many library managers do not make deliberate decisions concerning the appropriate match between their employees and public contact requirements. However there are fundamental issues of motivation and competency that managers should address in hiring and in developing and training staff. These issues involve four major areas and related abilities:

Customer service: Responsiveness to customer requests whether or not the customer is visibly present, ability to put customers at ease in stressful situations, patience, and ability to solve problems both independently and as part of a team

Oral communication: Good listening skills and ability to clearly communicate concerns and information so that understanding is reached

Pressure and adaptability: Ability to handle multiple requests, multitasking; toleration of stress and frustration; adaptability to changing work conditions; and ability to deal with crises

Interpersonal sensitivity: Responsiveness to customer concerns, ability to calm down upset customers, respect for coworkers' responsibilities and priorities, and assertiveness, not aggressiveness[14]

Libraries are very much staff-intensive organizations. Approximately 70 percent of a library budget is consumed by staff cost. Therefore, the ability of a library to become a customer-centered quality operation rests *directly* upon the people that work there. When managers recognize the direct connection between staff and service, provide appropriate and sufficient training and staff development, and reward a service attitude, then the probability of higher levels of quality and customer satisfaction rises significantly. Truly, the customer is "always right" and does have the final word. Unless libraries provide staff at the front lines that recognize and respond to customer needs, customers will still vote with their feet—and find information elsewhere.

Measuring Customer Satisfaction

How can we measure customer perception of value? William A. Band, author of *Creating Value for Customers,* proposes that there are certain basic principles that should be incorporated into any research on customer satisfaction.[15] These are rephrased in terms of library operations. That is, any research on library customers should

focus on customer expectations (the quality and type of service or product customers expect to receive) and on customer perceptions (what customers believe they are receiving), not on what the library thinks it is delivering

focus on the quality of the product or service

involve library staff in developing customer satisfaction measures and criteria by using strategies such as focus groups, staff workshops, and staff surveys

include both qualitative and quantitative data

develop questions for surveys or interviews that are specific and easy to collect and record

be designed so that managers or staff can take action or implement change based on the results; therefore, questions should be written in measurable terms

ensure that rewards for bringing about positive change based on the results of the customer research are visible and valuable

As with all research efforts, you should identify and adapt suitable models successfully used by other libraries and organizations. Sample surveys can be found in Band's work and in other management titles. Whether the specific research tool selected is a telephone survey, a mail survey, in-person interviews, focus groups, or customer comment cards and a suggestion box (to name some popular tools), base the selection on local conditions and the data needed for decision making. The choice will depend on the target markets, geographical area, complexity and quantity of information sought, timeline over which the data must be collected, and funds available for the effort.

Before you attempt any research, however, some clearly defined planning and problem-solving programs must be in place. Chapters 4 and 5 will address the formation of teams and the process of problem solving in more detail.

▪ 2 ▪

The Reference Desk

Susan is staffing the reference desk when a customer approaches. Susan raises her eyes and smiles a warm welcome. The customer hesitates, then asks a brief question that is somewhat vague. In her best customer-service style, Susan begins to ask a series of questions to more accurately pinpoint the true nature of the question. A second customer walks up and stands patiently in line, followed by a third customer. Suddenly, the telephone rings. The first customer looks somewhat startled. The telephone rings again, more insistently. In all probability, there is yet another customer at the other end of the telephone line.

What should Susan do?

One Possible Response

Susan asks the first customer to excuse her for a moment, explaining to the other customers in line that she will be with them in a few minutes. She answers the telephone and explains to that customer that she is busy with another customer. She takes down the customer's telephone number and promises to return the call within a few minutes. Susan returns her attention to the first customer and responds to the reference request. When this first transaction is completed, Susan turns to the waiting customers. Another customer has joined the line, and Susan explains to that customer that she must return a prior telephone call but will be available in just a few minutes.

Questions to Consider

- Which customer has priority? Why?
- Do telephone inquiries have equal weight in importance with the customer standing before the reference desk?
- Should the telephone customer have been asked to hold?
- Should the telephone question have been answered immediately and the present customer delayed? Why or why not?

Is there a better way to handle this situation? You decide.

Notes

1. Warren Blanding, *Practical Handbook of Customer Service Operations: Translating Excellence into Action* (Washington, D.C.: International Thomson Transport Pr., 1989), 23.

2. Roger Gould, *Transformations: Growth and Change in Adult Life* (New York: Simon & Schuster, 1978). Daniel J. Levinson, and others, *The Seasons of a Man's Life* (New York: Knopf, 1978). George E. Vaillant, *Adaptation to Life: How the Best and the Brightest Came of Age* (Boston: Little, Brown, 1977). Erik H. Erikson, *Childhood and Society*, 2d ed. (New York: Norton, 1963); *Identity: Youth and Crisis* (New York: Norton, 1968). Bernice Neugarten, ed., *Middle Age and Aging* (Chicago: Univ. of Chicago Pr., 1966).

3. Gail Sheehy, *Passages: Predictable Crises of Adult Life* (New York: Hart, 1972); *New Passages: Mapping Your Life Across Time* (New York: Random, 1995).

4. Russell D. Robinson, *An Introduction to Helping Adults Learn and Change* (Milwaukee, Wisc.: Omnibook, 1979), 16–20.

5. Gail Sheehy, "45 Ain't What It Used to Be as Life Cycle Shifts," *The Capital Times* (Sept. 23, 1995), 3D.

6. Karl Albrecht, *The Only Thing That Matters: Bringing the Power of the Customer into the Center of Your Business* (New York: Harper, 1992), 128–9.

7. William H. Davidow and Bro Uttal, *Total Customer Service: The Ultimate Weapon* (New York: Harper, 1989), 153.

8. Michael Buckland, *Redesigning Library Services: A Manifesto* (Chicago: ALA, 1992), 62.

9. Davidow and Uttal, 13.

10. William A. Band, *Creating Value for Customers* (New York: Wiley, 1991), 25.

11. Band, 25.

12. Benjamin Schneider and David E. Bowen, *Winning the Service Game* (Boston: Harvard Bus. School Pr., 1995), 112.

13. Schneider and Bowen, 112.

14. Schneider and Bowen, 123.

15. Band, 77–9.

3

What Is Excellence?

Libraries were once the major players in the information industry, dominating the field for centuries. Today, however, libraries are but one group of players in competition with increasing numbers of others, such as vendors, publishers, media and multimedia producers, mass media, online services, the Internet, and the World Wide Web. This competitive environment has the potential for becoming increasingly hostile and demanding. Each player is seeking a unique market niche and a competitive edge. Service quality can provide that advantage.

In chapter 1, the following equation was presented:

$$\frac{E \times X^{CE}}{CN + CS} = S + P$$

It graphically illustrated the question, "How can the library create and maintain *excellence* in a *changing environment* where responding to *customer needs* and focusing on *customer satisfaction* determines *survival* and *prosperity?*" Both chapters 1 and 2 addressed elements of the changing environment, with an emphasis on the customer serving as the focus of chapter 2. The one missing piece from the left side of this equation is *excellence,* which is the topic of this chapter.

The Complexity of Excellence and Quality

Why is excellence important to customer service? While the shifting sands of the environment pose continuing challenges and customer needs are also dynamic in nature, excellence contains the attributes of both *movement* and *stability.* No service can be considered truly excellent unless the products offered meet standards of high quality. However, quality is determined by internal traits such as product condition, accuracy, and reliability—and by the changing characteristics of timeliness and convenience.

Quality can be regarded as a moving target. Obviously, library materials that are in need of repair, are out-of-date, or have incorrect information do not meet even a mediocre standard. Information secured as the result of a reference interview and subsequent research may be less easily verified, but the importance of accuracy and reliability is no less essential. Therefore, the intrinsic worth of the physical object or informational response carries considerable weight in assessing quality.

If the internal quality of either tangible or intangible communication is assessed to meet high standards, this is only the beginning. Band, in his far-reaching work, *Creating Value for Customers,* attempts to examine quality through several lenses:

Transcendent quality: An innate beauty and excellence as the means to customer satisfaction

Product-based quality: Quality that is measurable and to a high standard; customer satisfaction is achieved by having more of some element or attribute

User-based quality: Only the customer can be the judge of what quality is; users' perceptions of how well their wants and needs are met

Operations-based quality: How closely the product meets the specifications set for it

Value-based quality: Conformance to requirements, including price and cost of production; meeting customer needs at a competitive price[1]

Clearly, these are very diverse lenses, and they demonstrate the complexity of the concept of quality. In addition, within any organization, various individuals may subscribe to one lens while other staff members prefer different lenses. To blend these approaches and arrive at a mutually acceptable definition of quality throughout the organization is a significant challenge, but one that must be addressed early in the search for excellence.

The Library's Products

When service excellence is the goal, the product itself is a logical starting point. Unlike the for-profit sector (where, admittedly, some information agencies reside), the concept of product is less well-defined in the not-for-profit world. This is the milieu in which most libraries operate, and the identities of the various library products are both tangible (the collection, bibliographies, pathfinders, research reports) and intangible (reference service, circulation, programs, readers' or learners' advisory, online services, interlibrary loan, information and referral).

Profit industries cost out their products by assessing the value of raw materials, labor, and overhead—plus a profit percentage. These calculations yield a per-unit cost that is then translated into a charge per sale. This is a cumulative process moving from the sum of a series of cost factors to a specific price assignment.

The library's products must be analyzed differently. Libraries typically receive a finite amount of funding that must then be allocated over a variety of cost centers. It is not possible to raise prices when the costs of materials and labor go up. Therefore, library managers are faced with an exercise in stewardship that is challenging and often frustrating. Consequently, to make product decisions that are also grounded in accountability to funding authorities, managers must carefully determine cost-benefit ratios relative to customer need and demand.[2]

To visualize the parameters of the term *product*, it is useful to begin with the definitions of Philip Kotler, author of *Marketing for Nonprofit Organizations.* Kotler has conceptualized the product in three levels or dimensions.

Product mix: The set of all product lines and items that a [library] makes available to its customers

Product line: A group of products within the product mix that are related by means of function, availability to the same customers, or marketed through the same outlets

Product item: A unit within a product line that is distinguishable by attributes such as size, appearance or price[3]

The relationship between these three dimensions is graphically illustrated in figure 3.1.

Figure 3.1   The Three-Dimensional Product Mix

	Product Mix Length		
	Collection	*Services*	*Programs*
Product Line Width	Books (30,000)	Circulation (100,000 items)	Film series (30)
	Periodicals (200)	Interlibrary loans (30,000 items)	Literacy tutoring (20 students)
	Videos (100)	Online searches (2,000)	Lecture series (10)
	CDs (300)		
	Audio books (200)		

While library directors or managers need to make decisions within the parameters of a finite budget, product decisions may be made within the dimensions of the product mix. In other words, it is possible to adjust the product profile in a number of ways:

lengthen the product mix by adding another product line (such as a gift shop or food service)

shorten the product mix by eliminating a category (such as programs) expand a product line by adding another format (such as computer software within the collection product line)

contract the product line by eliminating a format (such as hard copy periodicals within the collection line if CD-ROM versions will take their places)

increase the depth of a product line by increasing the number of individual product items (such as buying additional videos for the collection line)

Therefore, you need to recognize that there is flexibility within the not-for-profit model when making product decisions. (Psychologically, being aware that you can control product decisions, even when the winds of fiscal misfortune are blowing, can be reassuring.) While you may have to make unpopular or unpleasant decisions, at least the jurisdiction is internal to the library, not externally imposed.

Furthermore, when you link the process of product decision making to a program budget, the effect of each product decision can be easily documented. This kind of documentation provides clear evidence of library programmatic directions—and funding consequences—to both customers and funding authorities and can often help reverse a negative budget determination. The ability to substantiate budget requests is a managerial imperative and is critical to product outcomes.

Intangibles and the Augmented Product

The product just described is portrayed in a way that is both simple and basic. The concept of product is actually much more complex and involves a series of levels and related factors. One way to display the qualities inherent in this concept of product can be found in figure 3.2. In this model, there is a core product, a tangible product, and an augmented product.[4] The core product answers the question *What is the customer really seeking?*

In Scenario 3 the core product would be information concerning France and the French language. The core product is always made available to the customer in some tangible form; in

Figure 3.2   Product Qualities

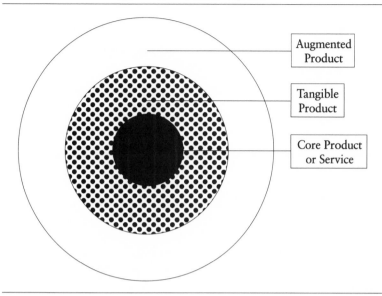

this case, travel books, French language books, audiotapes, and videotapes. Tangible products have up to five characteristics:

> *Features:* The content is designed for the beginner, intermediate, or advanced student

---

SCENARIO 3

A Visit to France

A young woman enters the library seeking to satisfy a need to learn French before going on a vacation to France. The librarian supplies travel books, French language books, audiotapes of French for travelers, and videotapes of France and Paris. The customer is very pleased with the helpfulness of the staff, the cheerful attitude with which she is greeted, the condition and currency of the materials supplied, the speed with which additional items not onsite can be secured, and the offer to put her in touch with some students from France who are staying with families in the area.

Packaging: Books, audiotapes, videotapes, and computer programs

Styling: The package is colorful, well-designed, and appealing

Quality level: The physical condition and accuracy range anywhere from excellent to poor

Brand name: Reputation of the publisher or producer[5]

Finally, the library can offer additional services and benefits to the customer that go beyond the tangible product, thereby producing an augmented product.[6] Such services might include audiotape or videotape players or computers for use in the library or available to be checked out, referral to a member of the community willing to tutor students in French, and referral to adult education classes in French. Other illustrations of augmentation can include the friendliness of staff, the speed at which materials are secured if not immediately available, telephone renewal of materials, and extended checkouts for travelers.

This example demonstrates the complex nature of the library product and the interrelatedness of the three product levels. The simple answering of a reference question is, therefore, not as simple as it may be perceived. Several processes and forces come into play within the delivery of any product to the customer, and care must be taken to ensure a high level of quality in all product aspects.

Atmospherics and the Library Environment

The multilayered product described cannot and does not exist in a vacuum. Rather, it resides within an environment that also shapes and colors the product itself. Kotler describes atmospherics as "the conscious designing of space to create or reinforce specific effects on buyers, such as feelings of well-being, or safety, or intimacy, or awe."[7] The following points illustrate the four decisions that need to be made regarding physical space:

What should your library look like on the outside? Should it reflect the architecture of its neighborhood or be distinctive? Should a lot of glass be used in its design? Should the overall effect inspire reverence, approachability, or practicality? This decision must be influenced by the message that the library wants to send to the community.

What should be the functional and flow characteristics of your building? What signage is necessary to guide customers to the various parts of the collection? What are the needs of the staff for handling customers and materials efficiently? Can customers locate and use materials without wandering aimlessly? Are professional staff easily identified?

What should your library feel like on the inside? Every building conveys a feeling, whether intentionally planned or not. Do you want your library to feel somber and traditional? Light and airy? Homey and comfortable? Modern and on the cutting edge?

What interior conditions would best support the desired feeling of your library? These conditions include visual cues (color, brightness, furniture arrangement, lighting), aural cues (quiet areas, active areas), olfactory cues (scent, freshness), and tactile cues (temperature, upholstery textures, carpet or tile).[8]

The look and feel of a library have direct effects upon both customers and staff and, ultimately, upon customer satisfaction and employee performance. If limited funds are available, small changes can dramatically change the overall feeling of a library. Even minor adjustments are appreciated and welcomed. What kinds of minor steps can improve the comfort or effectiveness of a library? For example:

signage that is visible, colorful, and easy to interpret

routine weeding to keep shelves from looking overcrowded

light-colored walls and flooring kept clean and fresh and as new-looking as possible

bright, interesting, and well-maintained bulletin boards and displays

adequate lighting and heating, ventilation, and air-conditioning

an uncluttered appearance overall

furniture that looks comfortable and is arranged for use

work surfaces that are at appropriate heights for the assigned tasks

Of course, there are many more possibilities—bounded only by the creativity of the library staff. To repeat a former point: staff cost is the largest item in the library's budget. The flip side of that statement could read: staff-customer interaction has the greatest effect on customer satisfaction.

Does a Smile Equal Good Service?

Customer satisfaction implies a complete fulfillment of one's wishes, needs, and expectations.[9] Unless the sole reason for interacting with library staff is one of pleasant social interaction, the ingredient of cheerful staff (while important) cannot alone constitute total satisfaction. In fact, the satisfaction quotient necessarily includes the following components:

contribution to fulfillment of the customer's goals for the use of the information or materials

fulfillment of the customer's specific wishes, needs, and expectations

customer anticipation that future needs will also be met

These components are essential attributes of customer satisfaction. However, a smile is not irrelevant; staff attitude is integral to the service rendered. As discussed previously, the product essence goes far beyond the core information. The excellence of the augmented product includes by definition the demeanor and degree of helpfulness staff members exhibit.

Therefore, in one sense, a smile does equal good service, and service will be diminished by its absence. Yet, customer satisfaction is a much larger issue. In addition to the components listed, Dick Berry, author of *Managing Service for Results*, cites four elements that characterize customer satisfaction: intensity, congruence, ambiguity, and periodicity.[10] Translating these elements into the library setting can clarify their centrality to the concept of customer satisfaction.

Intensity: A measure of the value of a product attribute or service activity to a customer. While admittedly tied to personal and individual customer reaction, intensity can be illustrated by the perceived value of information secured by computer access to the library's catalog during hours when the library is closed—as contrasted with information secured by telephoning the library during open hours and waiting one's turn in a reference queue.

Congruence: A measure of the difference between actual and expected levels of satisfaction. Before contacting the library, the customer may have preconceived expectations of what the library can provide. After receiving service, these expectations may be unrealized, met, or exceeded.

Ambiguity: A measure of how clearly the customer can relate satisfaction to a product or service. After receiving notification from the library that a desired book is available, the customer may be unaware of the succession of steps taken to secure that material. The level of ambiguity can be lowered by staff explanation of how materials are accessed from distant locations.

Periodicity: A measure of the frequency with which a customer experiences satisfaction or dissatisfaction. If a customer receives excellent service one time and poor or inadequate service on another occasion, the inconsistency of interaction with the library leads to lower satisfaction and expectation.

In light of this discussion, it becomes evident that excellence is a moving target and that what is excellent service today may be less than adequate service tomorrow. As society and technology undergo transformational change, customers' expectations shift in like manner. Therefore, it is a challenge to library staff to continually strive to provide excellent products and service in an "Alice in Wonderland" world in which the definitions are forever under review.

■ 3 ■

The Case of the Obsolete Atlas

A customer enters the library and walks over to the reference section. Standing before the case containing various atlases, he carefully looks through an atlas of the world. After a few moments, he turns abruptly and marches over to the reference desk.

Adrian asks the man if he can be of assistance. The customer states curtly that he is trying to locate a certain city in an African country and finds that the atlas is badly out of date. He claims that a number of African countries have undergone name changes since the atlas was printed. In a raised voice, he denounces the library for having such an out-of-date atlas in its collection.

Several customers are seated at nearby tables. They look up to see what the commotion is all about.

How should Adrian handle this situation?

One Possible Response

Adrian assures the customer that he will give the atlas to the library director for replacement and apologizes for any inconvenience. Since there is not another, more current, atlas immediately available, Adrian telephones another library to get the information needed by the customer.

Questions to Consider

- What can Adrian do to regain this customer's business?
- Does/should the library's collection policy have clear statements concerning replacement of materials?
- What procedures should the library have in place to trigger when an item becomes obsolete?
- What can the library do to recapture the trust of the customers who were "listening in"?

Is there a better way to handle this situation? You decide.

Notes

1. William A. Band, *Creating Value for Customers: Designing and Implementing a Total Corporate Strategy* (New York: Wiley, 1991), 145–8.

2. Darlene E. Weingand, *Marketing/Planning Library and Information Services* (Littleton, Colo.: Libraries Unltd., 1987), 57.

3. Philip Kotler, *Marketing for Nonprofit Organizations,* 2d ed. (Englewood Cliffs, N.J.: Prentice-Hall, 1982), 289.

4. Kotler, 291–6.

5. Philip Kotler and Alan R. Andreasen, *Strategic Marketing for Nonprofit Organizations,* 3d ed. (Englewood Cliffs, N.J.: Prentice-Hall, 1987), 423–7.

6. Kotler and Andreasen, 423–7.

7. Kotler, 325–6.

8. Adapted from Kotler, 326.

9. Dick Berry, *Managing Service for Results* (Research Triangle Park, N.C.: Instrument Soc. of America, 1983), 141.

10. Berry, 147.

4

The Team Approach

Customer service can be handled on a one-to-one basis and, indeed, must be viewed by each staff member as a personal responsibility. However, the intent of this chapter is to extend the customer service mandate beyond the individual to teams and team building. While an individual can make every effort to provide good customer service, this good work may not be integrated into the organization. By creating teams that are given the charge to develop a process that will lead to improved customer service and by providing management support, you send a clear message to the entire library staff.

Improving Customer Service with Teams

Of course, teams can be charged with tasks that involve any aspect of the full spectrum of library operations. However, it is the purpose of this chapter to link the process of team building and team self-direction with the intent of improving customer service. While many library managers and staff mouth a philosophy of good service, in reality many of them have lost sight of this objective. In some libraries the organizational climate is such that employees are expected to work independently—to do a good job, to be sure, but to do so as individuals. Such an environment tends to de-emphasize more-coordinated efforts and the will to create strong relationships with customers.

Because there is a fundamental belief among library staff that service is the keystone of library operations, it can be difficult to accept the fact that customer service needs upgrading. Too often, daily tasks and repetitive crises—augmented by internal politics and personality clashes—absorb the attention of both management and employees. It is in this type of situation that fostering teamwork can be most challenging—and yet such efforts will make the most difference. Breaking loose from the paralysis of an internal focus is admittedly difficult, but the results can be strikingly dramatic.

The overall playing field in the workplace is one of required interdependence between staff and customers. No library can exist without customers. Conversely, customers require library staff and materials to address their informational and educational needs. However, even though this interdependence is a mandate for the library's existence, there are multiple ways that individual staff members can experience and manage it. Three major options for individual behavior include[1]

> *Independent work:* I mind my own business and take pride in doing a good job. I feel isolated in my work at the library and look elsewhere for my social interactions. I am careful to do the duties specified in my job description. (This is the classic example of "It's not in my job description" mentality, a negative force that disrupts harmony in the workplace. While a difficult challenge, such an employee must be made to realize the personal and organizational benefits presented by cooperation—or be counseled to seek employment elsewhere.)

> *Competitive stance:* Organizational rewards go to the winner, and I am in competition with other library employees. I have difficulty trusting other employees and I don't want to depend on others. I want to prove that I am more worthy than others. (This is a clear opportunity for

a redefinition of the library's reward structures and the development of a system that will compensate employees for cooperative efforts.)

Cooperative team: I am part of a team in which we all contribute to being as effective as possible. I depend on my team colleagues for support, encouragement, and information. We have good communication and look for solutions that are mutually beneficial. I am loyal both to my library and to my team.

Depending on their structure and management support, library teams can transform customer service or have no effect on customers whatever (see Scenario 4). In addition, because individual staff members can—and often do—react differently, training is an essential first step before teams are assigned. An interdependent work environment that fully endorses customer service does not occur spontaneously. Individuals must learn team behavior; enthusiastic embrace of change is native in only a small percentage of people. A true appreciation of interdependence is not easily achieved, but the results are well worth the effort.

Once interdependence as a philosophy has permeated the library's work ethic, translating intent into everyday reality is a critical next step. The depth of this interdependence can often be measured in terms of customer service. Certainly, the library is not the only way potential customers can satisfy their need for information or entertainment. In fact, their use or nonuse of the library may well depend upon the level of customer service provided.

Customer service can be perceived as visible and/or invisible. Visible customer service can be attributed to the qualities of accuracy, speed, and convenience—served up with a generous dose of helpfulness and cheerfulness. Invisible elements include those processes, procedures, and policies that are set in place to facilitate visible service, such as convenient hours, computerized access to the library's collection, faxed journal articles, extended circulation periods with easy renewals, adequate parking, and a delivery system that facilitates rapid interlibrary loans. Whether visible or invisible, the centerpoint of library operations rests squarely on the customer.

Forming Teams: Toward an Improved Organization

Transforming the library into an organization in which staff members feel responsible for and involved in the library's success is an effective approach to management and to good customer service. The "triple play" of good leadership, appropriately structured work, and suitable management practices can help to achieve this goal.[2] All three of these strategies can be found in the team approach to problem solving and decision making.

Employee involvement, including management practices that provide for involvement, has a significant positive effect on organizational effectiveness. Creating this organizational environment involves making choices that allow and encourage staff to know more, do more, and contribute more. These choices include information, power, knowledge, and rewards.[3]

> Information is shared among all staff members so that everyone is aware of areas of challenge and opportunity. Managers who keep staff informed will benefit from access to a larger pool of ideas and collaborative problem solving.

> Power, like love, increases when given away. Power that is hoarded tends to atrophy; power that is freely given empowers both the giver and the receiver.

> Knowledge leads to the generation of ideas and an increased sense of ownership. Staff members who are knowledgeable concerning the library's community, vision, mission, goals, and objectives—the planning and marketing processes of the library—can better design improved customer service strategies.

> Rewards need to be plentiful and dispensed often. Staff members who are displaying excellent customer service deserve to be recognized for their achievements.

Library directors who entertain the notion of forming teams to explore ways to improve customer service may be entering into uncharted territory. If the library staff already has experience with working on teams, this new endeavor may simply be a different charge. But if working on teams will be a new experience, then a good training foundation needs to be put in place, and the four areas cited above should be reassessed in terms of present operations and hoped-for results. In a team scenario, information, power, knowledge, and rewards need to be nurtured and widely shared. Traditional authoritarian structures will not produce positive results; employee involvement requires full participative management.

However, an emphasis on the "what" of forming teams is only part of the team development process. An emphasis must be placed on the people who will be the substance of those teams and how and why they will work together. The "who" component should involve representation from groups that will be affected by the decisions that will be made. "How" and "why" are more-complex questions. Will the team be permanent and continually monitor customer service practices, or will it be a short-term entity that develops and recommends customer service strategies and then phases out? Both of these models can work, and depending on the library's present organizational structure, one type may be preferable.

Regardless of present library structure—both internally and in terms of the external parent organization—the use of a team to assess present and potential customer service ideas will promote a sense of ownership and increase the number of ideas that a group brings to problem solving. In addition, Thomas J. Peters and Robert H. Waterman, authors of *In Search of Excellence,* found that "Our research told us that any intelligent approach to organizing had to encompass, and treat as interdependent, at least seven variables: structure, strategy, people, management style, systems and procedures, guiding concepts and shared values (i.e., culture), and the present and hoped-for corporate strengths or skills."[4] Using these variables as a point of departure for this discussion of team building, it is possible to develop teams around a customer service focus. The following sections elaborate upon these variables in a library setting.

Structure

Organizational structure clearly sets the tone for how the library will function. If the library has a history of hierarchical management with the director at the apex of the pyramid and other positions slotted into a rigid reporting/supervisory configuration, there is little chance that the team approach will be able to function independently. Such organizations create a climate that seeks to maximize control rather than involvement. Moreover, if teams are assigned to work on a problem, it is likely that they will be fact-finding in nature, and decision making still will rest with the traditional managers. However, if the library has experimented with more-dynamic structures, such as the orbit (see figure 4.1) or matrix (see figure 4.2) models, then the team model is already under way.

Figure 4.1   The Orbit Model

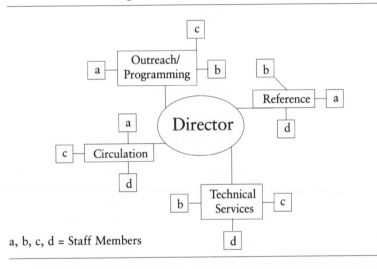

a, b, c, d = Staff Members

In figure 4.1, the director remains at the center of library functions, and the functions orbit the director's position. Staff members assigned to each function orbit that function, and the team leader position rotates among them. In the matrix model, figure 4.2, functions are divided into tasks. Each librarian serves as team leader for one responsibility and as a team member for others. These structures support employee involvement in organizational operations and an orientation that fosters increased individual commitment. Team interaction can then build upon this increased commitment and involvement. The development of these models can be part of permanent organizational restructuring or can be developed as a design for a short-term project that focuses on improving customer service.

Figure 4.2   The Matrix Model

Assigned Teams

Task 1	A	d	c	f
Task 2	B	f	d	e
Task 3	C	e	b	a
Task 4	D	c	f	b
Task 5	E	b	a	d
Task 6	F	a	e	c

A, B, C, D, E, F = Task Leaders

a, b, c, d, e, f = Team Members

Strategy

The strategy to be used in appointing teams and delivering the charges will vary according to the mix of the rest of the variables. An assessment of the strengths and limitations of each variable should drive the management-decision process. All team members are entitled to know exactly how the team is to operate. Depending on the management style of the library director, the team will be expected to gather data and function within one of the following models:

all decisions are made by the library director

the team submits recommendations; decisions are made by the library director

the team makes recommendations and ultimately shares in making the decisions

In addition, managerial credibility is essential to the team process. If management has a history of forming teams, receiving results, and filing those results away without taking action, team members will be far less likely to take the team process seriously. If, however, management routinely takes all team results under consideration and gives feedback to the team, the entire process is empowered. This does not imply that all team recommendations must go forward into an implementation phase; rather, the reasons why they are—or are not—implemented are clearly communicated to team members.

People

The members of a team are critical to the functioning and ultimate success of the team effort. It is important to once again restate that there should be representation on the team from groups that will be affected by the decisions to be taken. In terms of customer service, the composition of the team should include staff from various levels or departments and with various responsibilities in the library. To understand the personality mix of potential team members, the library manager may wish to consider having staff members take the Myers-Briggs (MBTI) instrument.[5] The MBTI has many advantages:

> It identifies and highlights the personality strengths of each person.
>
> All results are positive and affirming—no result is regarded as superior to another.
>
> It can only be administered and interpreted by a trained leader.
>
> It allows the library director to form teams based on an appropriate mixture of individual attributes. In other words, a team composed of members holding similar personality characteristics may not be as effective as a team reflecting a balance of different personality types.

To adapt a well-used maxim: the whole can indeed be greater than the sum of its parts. The mix of personalities and experiences that a team brings to the process of problem solving can provide very valuable depth and insights. While teamwork generally takes more time in the short term, in the long term there is likely to be greater "buy-in" and commitment to the customer service decisions that emerge.

Management Style

There are many variations of management style ranging along a continuum from the highly authoritarian to the other pole of full staff participation. Management style will have a very strong impact on team formation, behavior, and output. A library manager who tends to operate toward the authoritarian pole of an administration continuum may be totally uninterested in using teams at all; in fact, a high level of interest in improving customer service may also be absent. However, a manager who believes in participatory management will embrace the concept of team building and seek to share the decision-making responsibility with team members; the goal of excellence in customer service is likely also to be embraced.

Systems and Procedures

The effort to improve customer service through the use of teams requires that the most effective team-building techniques be put into place. Many factors contribute to team building and operation. Some useful tactics include

Identification of present and hoped-for corporate strengths: What are the library's current strengths—and limitations? What goals are in place? What would the library look like in an ideal world? A team cannot operate in a vacuum. To generate ideas that will move the library forward, a clear picture of the "now" is critical—and this self-portrait must be candid and honest.

Team size and composition: As introduced in "Goldilocks and the Three Bears," size can be "too big," "too small," or "just right." A "just right" size for working effectively in teams is somewhere between five and nine members drawn from management, staff, and targeted customer groups.

Team charge and expectations: Why is the team being established? What are its responsibilities? What is the timeline? Will the team be collecting data, making recommendations, and making decisions or some combination of these tasks? What is the hoped-for outcome of its efforts? A team needs to have clear direction and shared values if customer service is to be improved.

Team support: For a team to operate efficiently, support measures need to be in place. For example, logistical support is essential. Someone from the library staff should be designated to arrange meetings, take minutes, do necessary photocopying, and so forth. Administrative support regarding release time and reassignment of normal duties is definitely a plus.

Operating climate: Ground rules need to be set, including a mandate for mutual respect of team members and their ideas. Group training can help team members work effectively within the team structure. In addition, they should receive some training in working positively with change because change can be difficult for some staff to accept.

Nominal group technique: This method enables all good ideas to be presented; it levels the playing field between the very vocal and the more-reticent team members. All team members silently write down all their ideas regarding a designated topic, such as "how to decrease the amount of time between the issuance of a request and the delivery of materials or information." When all ideas have been written down, each team member (one at a time) states one idea, and it is then written on a flip chart. Each team member is polled in turn and the circuit is continued until all ideas have been placed on the flip chart and numbered. No judgments as to the merits of an idea are allowed at this point.

Once all ideas are collected, the team members are instructed to "choose their favorite five." Once again, the team is polled and tally marks are placed next to each idea selected. The top "vote-getting" ideas are to be considered first by the team; however, all ideas are retained for future discussions.[6]

Administrative Supports

Once one or more teams have been created, the following questions must be asked:

In terms of customer service, how is the library doing?

Where does the library stand vis-a-vis philosophy, daily effort, policies, and staff commitment?

What needs to happen for the library to focus more completely on the customer?

Incorporate these questions into the charge given to the newly formed team. However, preparing the charge is only the first step in providing administrative support so that the team can function independently and effectively. The kind and amount of administrative supports that drive the team effort send a clear message about how seriously the library manager takes the venture. What types of support are needed by the team? A starting point includes some or all of the following:

   release time from normal duties

   reassignment of some normal duties so that sufficient time is available within the workday for team meetings and activities

   fiscal, human, equipment, and supply resources

   clerical assistance

   ongoing communication and feedback with management, library staff, and customers

If "a picture is worth a thousand words," then the allocation of sufficient resources in support of the team effort speaks louder than all the press releases and oral pronouncements that management might care to make.

   With adequate supports in place, the goal, from an administrative point of view, involves a series of outcomes: the team(s) will

   cooperate and work well together

   work with available resources

   take initiative and suggest courses of action

   focus on team contributions rather than individual achievements

   focus on solutions rather than roadblocks or blame

   continually improve on preset expectations

   seek to innovate

   be proactive rather than reacting to crises

   improve quality

The closer the library director's management style is to the participative pole of the continuum, the more readily a team can develop a self-directed work ethic. An environment of staff involvement, if already present, can easily be translated into a team model. It is when the authoritarian and hierarchical style is dominant that more preliminary work—and training—needs to be done to set the stage for teamwork. (See Scenario 4.)

Integrating Customer Service into Library Operations

There are four basic tasks that the team must accomplish to switch to an external customer-oriented focus and to raise the level of customer service.

1. *It must reconcile the differences between how they want to serve customers and the present quality of service.*

    More is involved here than a simple desire to improve. The first step is an objective analysis of present service in the library, identifying areas of excellence as well as the location of less-than-adequate efforts. Step two is to determine the goal: an optimum service profile. Step three identifies the gaps between "what is" and "what should be." The final step determines what concrete actions can be taken to bridge those gaps.

2. *It must develop an organization united behind serving customers well.*

    Now that the plan for improving customer service is "on paper," it is time (or even past time!) to provide sufficient in-service training for the entire staff. Along with this training, the staff must analyze and restructure (as needed) the patterns of organizational communication to encourage multidirectional communication patterns. It will not be possible to achieve the desired organizational unity without freely moving lines of communication. Every staff member needs to be able to believe in—and restate when asked—the library's mission, goals, and objectives. All employees must be "on the same page" if a concentrated effort toward improving customer service is to succeed.

SCENARIO 4

Transforming Teams into Stakeholders

Team Attribute	Library A	Library B
Size and composition	Ten; staff and board members	Seventeen; representatives from all identified constituent groups, external and internal; subdivided into task forces
Charge to the team	Unclear; poor history of using teams and committees well	Well-defined; expectations shared by all team members
Library strengths and limitations	Vague and ill-defined	Clearly identified through staff survey
Administrative support	Verbal; no resources allocated	Verbal and written; sufficient resources allocated
Communication	Dominated by a few team members	All viewpoints presented; nominal group and other strategies introduced
Reporting	Team report received and filed	Team report accepted and communicated to internal and external target markets; administration consults with team members and clearly explains what can be done immediately, what must be tabled, what cannot be done and why

Which library will be most successful in using teams? Why?

3. *It must lay the groundwork for employees to develop solid relationships with customers.*

How can this be done? Time and time again, the answer lies in training—training that is endorsed and nurtured by administrative support. This training should provide both *vision* and *permission*: the vision that paints a picture of how excellence in customer service can benefit the library and staff members as well as customers and the permission to let go of prior attitudes and beliefs in the journey toward new, unfamiliar, and uncharted service capabilities. This training must be brought into balance with the library's reward system because employees will not take training concepts seriously if the reward system is sending a different message.

4. *It must manage conflict and refine skills to continuously develop and improve the organization's ability to serve customers.*

Effective conflict resolution will be a key success factor. Different staff members will inevitably exhibit varying levels of acceptance and may display both frustration and hostility. However, in diversity lies strength. If these negative expressions can be turned around, the staff ownership of the entire process will increase in intensity.[7]

These four tasks, once accomplished, smooth the way for the integration of customer service into normal day-to-day library operations. This is a fundamental objective for customer service excellence. The process moves from planning where the library needs to go, to developing a supporting philosophy, to implementing the training/reward structure, and, finally, to managing the interpersonal skills that make customer service excellence possible. All four components of this process must be in place to make full integration possible.

Target: Long-Term Relationships— The Development of Stakeholders

Customer service is not a sometime or once-in-a-while thing. Like public relations, it is a relationship that is developed over long periods and requires consistency in both quantity and quality. If a customer receives excellent service on one occasion and poor treatment the next, his or her overall impression will probably lean toward the negative. Certainly, the customer will not develop a sense of overall excellence vis-a-vis library service. It is essential that the library staff commit to improved customer service and add two more steps to the four outlined above.

5. *It must execute front-line improvements.*

It is at the initial encounter between customer and library that the tone of customer service is established.

6. *It must build in a strategy of continuous improvements.*

In many ways, developing long-term stakeholder relationships is not dissimilar to running a race: a quick sprint can put an athlete out in front in the beginning, but it is continued effort that will sustain the lead throughout the race. When you institute a focus on improving customer service, an occasional "spurt" of effort will not achieve the goal. The library staff must *adopt the new standard of service as a minimum acceptable level,* while simultaneously working on a service design that will put in place a sequence of improvements. If relationships with customers are to improve over the long term, then a system of sustained effort is essential.

Long-term nurturing of the library–customer relationship has an outcome far beyond the obvious increase in customer satisfaction: the development of both internal and external stakeholders. While library staff might already have a vested interest in the well-being of the library, it is a significant benefit to staff when customers are satisfied. It is true that staff are obvious internal stakeholders in the present operations and future effectiveness of the library. However, when customers also become stakeholders—because the library has become essential to their quality of life—the involvement of the library in the life of the community escalates, and everyone benefits. Stakeholders do more than simply use the library: they *care* about its success, they promote its activities, and they are active *lobbyists* in its behalf.

The library's customer service team (or teams) needs to internalize this concept of developing stakeholders so that the long-range goal is in mind even as other goals are established and realized. There is no shortcut possible when stakeholder ownership is the primary motivation. Although complex and sometimes out of reach, this overarching goal can help keep the entire team-generated process on track.

Whether the team approach to improving customer service is developed as a "kick start" model or as a part of library reorganization, the use of teams can generate staff ownership, customer involvement, and a host of interactive thinking and planning that can speed the desire for continuous improvement in customer service on its way.

■ 4 ■

The Bipolar Team

The library is about to begin its very first planning effort, including a marketing audit. The library director and several staff members have completed some planning and marketing seminars and are enthusiastic about this new process. The director has assembled a planning team composed of representatives from staff, funders, policy-makers, community agencies, media, and various target markets. The first planning meeting is almost concluded, and some obvious problems have arisen.

Two of the team members have expressed strong opinions and tend to dominate the meeting. Other team members seem to be shy or, if not shy, decidedly intimidated by the more-vocal members. The library director serves as an ad hoc member of the team, and the team has elected a chairperson from among their number.

How can the team chairperson facilitate meetings
so that all members contribute?

One Possible Response

The chairperson has had experience with the nominal group technique (NGT) and uses this strategy to elicit ideas from each team member. By basing initial discussion within the parameters of the NGT, each member is encouraged to contribute as many ideas as possible, and judgment (by others) is suspended until all ideas have been collected.

Questions to Consider

- NGT is only one possible way to handle this group. What are others?
- How important is it to ensure that all team members contribute? Why?
- If a team is skewed in one direction, what are possible outcomes?
- Did the director do a good job of selecting people to serve on the team? Why or why not?

Is there a better way to handle this situation? You decide.

Notes

1. Dean Tjosvold, *Teamwork for Customers: Building Organizations that Take Pride in Serving* (San Francisco: Jossey-Bass, 1993), 5–6.

2. Edward E. Lawler III, *The Ultimate Advantage: Creating the High-Involvement Organization* (San Francisco: Jossey-Bass, 1992), 3.

3. Lawler, 4–5.

4. Thomas J. Peters and Robert H. Waterman Jr., *In Search of Excellence: Lessons from America's Best-Run Companies* (New York: Warner, 1982), 9.

5. I. B. Myers and M. H. McCaulley, *Manual: A Guide to the Development and Use of the Myers-Briggs Type Indicator* (Palo Alto, Calif.: Consulting Psychologists, 1985).

6. Adapted from Andrew H. Van de Ven and André L. Delbecq, "Nominal and Interacting Group Processes for Committee Decision-Making Effectiveness," *Academy of Management Journal* 14, no. 2 (June 1971): 203–12.

7. Tjosvold, xiv.

5

⚭

The Problem-Solving Process

Problem solving is an inevitable companion to improving customer service. If no problems were present, there would be no reason to be concerned about improving customer service—for staff dealings with customers would already be excellent. But such an ideal situation is not reality and no service-providing organization is without attendant problems. Moreover, whenever people interact with each other, problems will occur in communication, perceptions, and expectations.

In addition, working within a changing environment can virtually guarantee a sequence of problem situations. Today's library faces a series of continuing challenges brought about by evolving technologies, consumer desires, and shrinking funds. If excellence in customer service is to be a primary library goal, then problem solving must be viewed as a vital management and personnel skill.

A problem cannot exist, however, unless decision makers perceive a choice between at least two courses of action; dissatisfaction with a situation may exist, but it is a "problem" only when alternatives are possible. Before a problem can be solved, some decision maker must be dissatisfied and desire change.[1]

Determining if a situation is a problem is like interpreting whether a glass is half full or half empty. Viewing problems in the "half-full," optimistic way—as a challenge and an opportunity that can lead to better customer service—creates an organizational culture in which creativity can emerge and grow. However, library managers frequently operate in a crisis-oriented, reactive manner and focus on putting out "fires" as they occur. This is viewing the glass as half empty—a problem. Frequently, this approach results in temporary answers and not long-term solutions that could be found in a less-reactive approach. It is essential that long-term problem solving be conducted within the context of a strategic planning process that focuses on both issues and environmental scanning (seeking out projected trends).

The Link with Planning

Planning is often characterized in the literature as the quintessential purposive activity, incorporating target setting, problem solving, and a regular comparison of progress against goals.[2] Strategic planners resist the temptation to respond to immediate concerns on a daily basis, thereby diverting time and energy from viewing the larger picture. While today's operational difficulties do require attention, such decisions are developed as part of a strategic planning process and customer service policies. Undeniably, some managers will sacrifice the promise of future benefits on the premise that if today's customer service problems are not solved, they might personally not be around to experience tomorrow. Then there is the procrastinating manager who believes that proper planning cannot begin until immediate problems have been solved.

However, the diversity of interests found in practicing both daily problem solving and strategic planning can add to the stability of the overall process. Brett Sutton, author of *Public Library Planning*, states that there are four reasons for this.

1. Short-term problem solving in the context of long-range planning is a powerful motivator at every level of the

organization—and particularly for staff members who are not otherwise interested in thinking about the kind of abstract goals found in planning for customer service excellence.

2. Problems raised by staff members as part of the planning process are more public and, therefore, more difficult to ignore.

3. The act of reviewing problems from the more centralized, unstructured environment of long-range planning leads to the juxtaposition of diverse conditions and problems, thereby revealing patterns (of service behavior) that might otherwise not be seen.

4. The tendency for immediate problems to become entangled in the planning process is often viewed by staff members as a natural consequence of planning.[3]

Clearly, the benefits of linking problem solving with planning argue against addressing these processes separately. Further, the team-building strategies discussed in chapter 4 can be applied to planning. Teams formed to investigate how to improve customer service are ideally positioned for problem solving; problem solving then becomes an operational skill.

A Valuable and Necessary Skill

When you view problem solving not only as a process but as a springboard for decision making, it becomes linked to the negative pole where problems reside and to the positive pole of effective management practice. There are four distinguishable activities in the process of problem solving:

1. awareness or knowing that a problem exists
2. preparing to find a solution
3. attempting to produce a solution
4. evaluating the adequacy of the attempted solution[4]

The following nine steps are found in any research project, and problem solving incorporates the complementary skills required in research. The following research framework can be applied to the majority of customer service problems.[5]

1. *Define the management problem.*

   What customer service issues need to be resolved? This is the step in which preliminary solutions may be developed and tested.

2. *Set research objectives.*

   What data need to be collected? How will this data collection be carried out? How will the collected data contribute to the decision making that will address the identified customer service issues? Consider answering the following questions as part of this step:

   How satisfied are your customers with your products or services?

   What are the specific needs and expectations of each customer market? How important is each expectation to customer satisfaction?

   How well does your library meet customer expectations? How do you compare with competitive information providers in your service area?

   What are the biggest complaints or problems that customers have with your library? Which complaints are made the most frequently?

   Which complaints have the greatest potentially negative effect on customer satisfaction?

   How are your library and its products or services perceived and evaluated by key customer subgroups within your overall market area?

   What are your library's key strengths in satisfying customers? Key weaknesses? Greatest opportunities for improvement?

3. *Search for secondary data.*

   One of the central principles of problem solving and research is to gather together useful data that have already been collected. Examining the library's internal records is an obvious first step. This internal examination will yield three categories of information: data concerning the library's operations, data concerning customer usage, and data that identify the extent of the library's resources.

A second step is to research external sources of data, such as that gathered by government agencies at the local, state, and national levels; human services agencies; educational institutions; and professional associations. This external data can provide additional insights into customer characteristics and may help to explain customers' information-seeking behavior outside libraries. Also inspect online, Internet, and World Wide Web sources. When these secondary data are analyzed, you may need to redefine some of the research objectives and clarify the amount of resources available to the library to engage in data collection.

4. *Carry out exploratory research.*

Once the analysis of secondary data is completed, qualitative strategies such as focus groups or interviews with representatives of target markets can clarify the customer service issues identified. These qualitative strategies can provide additional insights into how present and potential customers seek information, view the library as an information resource, and perceive the present state of customer service in the library. To use interviews and focus groups, an interview schedule (similar to a questionnaire) must be developed so that important points are covered and the same questions or types of responses are requested of all participants. Sample items include

> What needs and expectations do you have for the library and its products and services?
>
> What are your biggest problems and complaints?
>
> How do you judge product and service quality?
>
> How would you compare the library relative to other information sources such as television, the Internet, video stores, and so forth?

Describe an incident in which you were served either very well or very poorly.

Potential target groups include funders, staff members, and representatives from identified customer groups.

5. *Plan the primary data-collection strategy.*

You must make several decisions at this stage:

How should the data be collected (mail survey, user study, telephone interviews, additional focus groups, etc.)?

From *whom* (which customer groups)?

What should be the *size* or extent of the survey?

How frequently should the collection be done?

A cautionary note must be added: Each library needs to determine the level of effort that it wishes to devote to this activity. Give consideration to the library's available resources: funding, personnel, time, and so forth.

6. *Design the customer-service research instrument.*

Develop the questionnaire or interview guide. Questionnaire design is a skill, and if the expertise is not available on your staff, seek it elsewhere. Designing a questionnaire that will elicit the hoped-for data is not a simple task and should not be attempted by amateurs without expert consultation. Mathematics, business, and statistics departments at local colleges, universities, and high schools are possible sources of professionals or students with the required expertise.

7. *Collect data.*

While it seems self-evident, it is necessary to once again emphasize that it can be devastating to overreach and collect so much data that staff are overburdened and wish never to repeat the process.

8. *Process and analyze data.*

Again, this is self-evident. But if the collection process has been scaled appropriately to available resources, the analysis phase will not feel like a hardship.

9. *Interpret and apply results.*

Analysis and interpretation are complementary, but not identical, activities. For example, if the data reveal that there are fifty small-business owners in the community and that a majority of these owners want the library to provide financial and stock market information, these are facts that have emerged from the data during analysis. Interpreting this information in relation to library resources may suggest that additional print materials, such as *Moody's* or *Thomas Register,* should be purchased— or if CD-ROM or Internet access may be more relevant to the library's customers. In other words, the data are evaluated relative to the customer service issues identified at the beginning of the process.

Library staff members must learn to function collaboratively in identifying and solving problems, and the library must develop institutionalized support and mechanisms for maintaining and improving these problem-solving processes. In short, this is a cooperative, action-research model for problem solving. In some cases, outside change agents are brought in to facilitate a sequence of activities.

Whatever the specific strategies, the staff tries to develop capabilities for problem solving. They also need procedures for scanning library operations. Such procedures should be designed to detect problems, diagnose them to determine changeable factors, and work toward collaboratively determined solutions.[6]

Reality Check: A Look at Paradigms

This entire problem-solving process is designed with the goal of collecting appropriate data to enhance decision making. However, we must recognize that there is a relationship between data and paradigms. A *paradigm* can be defined as a pattern or model that elicits behavior, together with the rules and regulations that we use to construct those patterns. We use these patterns to establish boundaries and ultimately to direct us on how to solve problems that lie within those boundaries.[7] In terms of customer service, the ways in which customers interact with the library are undergoing significant change, and the design of customer service policies and practice must also change.

Since paradigms influence our perceptions, it is important that this influence be truly appreciated. Joel A. Barker, a noted futurist, presents six important points:

1. Paradigms are common in all aspects of life.

2. Paradigms are useful; they show us what's important and what's not. They help us find important problems and go on to give us rules to help us solve the problems; they focus our attention.

3. Sometimes a paradigm can become *the* paradigm: the only way one can do something. When confronted with an alternative idea, we reject it out of hand.

4. The people who create new paradigms are usually outsiders; they are not part of the established paradigm community and are not invested in the old paradigm.

5. Those practitioners of the old paradigm who choose to change to the new paradigm early in its development are paradigm pioneers. They have to be very courageous; the evidence provided by the new paradigm does not prove that they should be changing.

6. You can choose to change the rules and regulations—shrug off one paradigm and adopt a new one.[8]

In customer service terms, an older paradigm would dictate that customers should use the library during normal hours of operation. To that end, the library has taken great pains to actively publicize its hours. However, a new paradigm would tell us that we should determine library hours with customer convenience and preferences in mind. In addition, we would recognize the central issue as one of *access* and not hours, and responding systems would be put in place (such as electronic access).

In Barker's view, changing a paradigm means fundamentally altering the way things are done and learning new ways to solve problems; standard ways of doing business become obsolete.[9] It may be that the concept of customer access is in need of radical redefinition. (See Scenario 5 for an example of a paradigm shift at an academic library.)

SCENARIO 5

Paradigm Shift in an Academic Library

Paradigm Attribute	Old Paradigm	New Paradigm
Access	Building with defined hours	Building with hours and access via computer
Collection	Primarily books and journals	Books, journals, CD-ROMs (networked) and accessible via computer dial-up or networks
Mission	To serve faculty, students, administrators; support of curriculum	Same—plus commitment to access through computer linkages and delivery systems
Staffing	Professionals, support staff, and students serving walk-in customers	Same—plus online and computerized assistance

Further, Barker states that paradigms act as filters that "screen" data coming into the mind, with the result that only data agreeing with the present paradigm has an easy path. Unexpected data that do not match the paradigm may be ignored. For example, data collected in a community survey may strongly indicate that customers prefer longer hours, weekend hours, and so forth. A staff member operating within the boundaries of the old paradigm may not "see" the data or, with his or her filter in place, may dismiss the finding as not relevant or possible in present economic circumstances. This is the "paradigm effect" in action, where the incoming data are screened and present expectations dominated by the old paradigm keep the staff from anticipating and preparing for the future. The result is "paradigm paralysis" and the status quo.

Barker poses the paradigm shift question and recommends referring to it often: "What today is impossible to do in your business, but if it could be done, would fundamentally change what you do?" Honest response to this question takes us to the boundaries of our present paradigms—the edge where the future may be anticipated.[10] While librarians do not necessarily need to be paradigm shifters, it is important that they learn to be "paradigm pioneers." The pioneer continually explores the boundaries of a present paradigm and, when a shift is first detected, becomes a risk taker who promulgates the transition from old to new. But in a global environment in which the rate of change is ever-increasing, the heaviest risk factors are switching from the pioneer to the late adopters; those who are not pioneers may find that, in seeking to move slowly and carefully, there may be no room for them because the paradigm is shifting once again.

The paradigm pioneer displays three primary characteristics:

A special kind of knowing, or intuition: an ability to make good decisions with incomplete information.

Courage: the willingness to move forward in the face of great risk.

Commitment of time: the time it takes to go from a rough concept to a working paradigm.[11]

Particularly in the information professions, the risks of not staying close to the edges of a present paradigm—the leading edge—are growing daily. Pioneers enter early—with hard work, long hours, great cleverness, and deep commitment to the long term—and drive the paradigm into practice.[12] Library staff that embrace the role of pioneer and believe in paradigm flexibility view problems as opportunities. Those hampered by paradigm paralysis perceive problems as threats. The friction between these two groups is known as *conflict*.

Managing Conflict

Conflict can have both a positive and negative effect on people who work together or on staff members and customers. It can be a boon when it stimulates provocative ideas, creative solutions, and zestful interchanges. It can become a bane, however, because it requires skill to make it constructive rather than destructive, calling on courage to face up to a problem and to work through to a resolution.[13]

Library managers approach problems and conflict in different ways. Toffler describes managers as being either "incrementalist" or "radical":

> One group assumes continuity; the other recognizes the growing importance of discontinuity.
>
> One group tends to formulate straight-line strategies; the other thinks in nonlinear terms.
>
> One tends to define problems cleanly, treating each as it comes along, more or less in isolation from the others. The second group tends to define problems less neatly but to see them in relationship to one another.
>
> One is good at "thinkable" solutions to problems—a leadership style that may be adequate in periods of environmental stability. The other is open to "unthinkable" solutions that may be necessary in periods of environmental turbulence.[14]

In the "real world," however, these are not two different groups but, rather, poles at either end of a continuum. In some situations, a manager's behavior may be closer to one pole than to the other. The degree of environmental stability—or lack of it—will influence how managers approach problems and conflict.

There are similarities between this continuum and the continuum that exists between leadership and management. On this latter continuum, the poles can be described as

> *Leadership:* The articulation of new values and the energetic presentation of them to those whose actions are affected by them
>
> *Management:* The discovery of value conflicts and the invention of processes for working them through[15]

Managers work toward greater harmony among the elements that are already present in the situation. Leaders change the elements. Each type of action is indispensable to the organization, depending upon the present environment. It is important to remember that, in some cases, leaders may not be managers and managers may not be leaders. This occurs when an individual operates very near one of the poles the majority of the time.

Managing the Emotional Side of Conflict

Conflict can be an intellectual activity, but in most cases, it includes a heavy dose of emotional involvement. Among the library's customers, emotion is generally felt as a variation of anger or frustration. What kinds of interaction with the library can produce these negative feelings? Figure 5.1 provides some common customer irritations.

Figure 5.1   Customer Frustration List

1. Customer is unable to locate materials or information.
2. Telephone is not answered promptly when customer calls.
3. Length of time until a reserved material is available seems too long.
4. Library staff is not friendly or helpful.
5. Library staff appears to be busy or unapproachable.
6. Parking is not available nearby.
7. Line at check-out is too long.
8. Librarian is not available to assist in locating material or information.
9. Customers are notified at inopportune times that requested items have arrived.
10. Library staff interpret policies literally and display a lack of flexibility.
11. Library hours are not convenient.
12. Customer must wait at the service desk while staff answers telephone.

What can be done to respond to these often unexpressed frustrations? The data collection discussed earlier should elicit responses that address some of the items on this list. At that time direct problem solving can take place. However, frustration that is felt but not expressed offers the deeper challenge.

Sheldon A. Davis, in discussing organizational change, expanded on the work of McGregor by stating that in dealing with each other, we will be open, direct, explicit. Our feelings will be available to each other, and we will try to *problem-solve* rather than be defensive.[16] This is a key concept because defensiveness lies at the heart of many conflicts. Particularly in terms of customer service, it is too easy to respond that "the library would like to be open more convenient hours . . . or provide connection to the Internet . . . or make the catalog available electronically (etc., etc.), but we don't have enough staff . . . money . . . time (etc., etc.)." Defensiveness leads to excuses, and excuses lead to inaction and apathy—or to confrontation. Consequently, customer service either gets worse or stays the same.

Confrontation, like crisis, has acquired a negative connotation. However, this interpretation is a distortion. Confrontation occurs when the discrepancy between two points of view is brought out into the open. Discrepancies generally occur in three areas: between the ideal state and the real state, between insight and actions, and between reality and illusions.[17] For example, if the check-out line is too long, the customer may be frustrated with the wait because she or he is already late for an appointment. The library's circulation clerk may believe that customers need to wait because the library does not have enough staff. What discrepancies might be present?

> In an ideal world, there would be no line. In the real world, lines do occur.
>
> The clerk may sense the customer's frustration but be unable to take action because no other staff member is presently available to assist. The customer may see that the clerk is alone, but believes that the library should put more people on circulation desk duty. This is a discrepancy between insight and actions.
>
> The reality of the situation is that the time spent in waiting is between 2 and 4 minutes. The illusion is that 5 to 10 minutes pass.
>
> Both parties may feel powerless to improve the situation.

Although confrontation is commonly expressed verbally, it can also be expressed physically: a hostile glare, toe or finger tapping, rude behavior, an upset stomach . . . the list goes on. When verbalized, it can be addressed; when suppressed, it will surface at another time or place that is removed from the provoking situation. How can the library staff manage potential confrontation with customers? Some remedies include

> a suggestion box placed in a prominent location
>
> customer surveys
>
> in-service training for staff in such areas as customer relations, communication, and body language

The list is definitely not all-inclusive. Further, any remedy involves some degree of *change*. Managing change requires the ability to identify the forces or variables surrounding a problem and then to develop consensus about them and a strategy of manipulating these forces.[18] Returning to the example, what might be some of the forces surrounding the problem of long lines at the circulation desk? One force has already been identified: inadequate staffing. How can this force be manipulated? Perhaps the staffing schedule can be rearranged to cover busy times better. Or the use of part-time staffing can be explored. Or an increased level of support staff can be written into the library's strategic plan. Creative brainstorming may uncover other possibilities. Whatever path is chosen, the important thing to recognize is that there are multiple paths—that is what problem solving is all about.

The Power of Communication

On the way to solving customer service problems, a selected path will lead into a maze without an exit *unless good communication skills are integral to the process.* Communication is like powerful medicine: a proper dose of correct ingredients can restore health; an improper dose or the wrong ingredients can produce ill effects. A variety of communication skills that are central to a smooth transfer of information and feelings will be discussed in detail in chapter 6.

Why is communication so important? Problem solving is a complex activity. Incorporated within the context of overall planning, supported by adequate data, considered in the context

of shifting paradigms, and enhanced by the skills of conflict resolution and communication, problem solving can become the keystone of continuously improving customer service. In summary,
if you

> acknowledge your customer's problem,
>
> carefully probe for information to clarify the scope of the
> problem,
>
> make sure that the customer is aware that you understand
> the problem,
>
> mutually look with your customer for alternative solutions,
>
> mutually agree on a plan to solve the problem, and
>
> follow up with your customer to make sure the problem is
> resolved,

then you have successfully engaged in a problem-solving process
that will strengthen your customer service. Congratulations!

Notes

1. Richard M. Dougherty and Fred J. Heinritz, "Scientific Management of Library Operations," in Beverly P. Lynch, *Management
   Strategies for Libraries* (New York: Neal-Schuman, 1985), 17.

2. Brett Sutton, *Public Library Planning: Case Studies for Management* (Westport, Conn.: Greenwood, 1995), 121–2.

3. Sutton, 123–4.

4. J. R. Kidd, *How Adults Learn* (New York: Association Pr., 1973),
   90.

5. William A. Band, *Creating Value for Customers* (New York:
   Wiley, 1991), 98–102.

6. Robert Chin and Kenneth D. Benne, "General Strategies for
   Effecting Changes in Human Systems," in Warren G. Bennis and
   others, *The Planning of Change*, 2d ed. (New York: Holt, 1969),
   47–8.

7. Joel A. Barker, *Paradigm Pioneers*, Discovering the Future Series
   (Burnsville, Minn.: Charthouse, 1993), video.

8. Joel A. Barker, *Discovering the Future: The Business of Paradigms*, 2d ed. (Burnsville, Minn.: Infinity Ltd. and Charthouse,
   1989), video.

▪ 5 ▪

The Angry Customer

The front door of the library slammed loudly, and the customer stomped up the stairs. In an angry voice, she demanded to see the library director. The circulation clerk attempted to calm the customer, but each effort seemed to aggravate the situation. Reluctantly, the clerk notified the director that the customer wished to see him.

In a few minutes, the director appeared and introduced himself to the customer. The customer began to recite her litany of complaints in a loud voice. Her complaints seemed to focus on the video that her son brought home from the library.

How should the director handle this situation?

One Possible Response

In a quiet and calming tone the library director suggests that the customer join him in the privacy of his office. He shows her to a comfortable chair and asks her to restate her comments, one at a time, so that he can respond. For each statement, which he carefully writes down, he repeats the statement back to the customer to be certain that he understands the customer's perspective. He is careful to affirm the customer's right to her opinion but offers relevant information when appropriate. Handing her a copy of the library's complaint and reconsideration form, he encourages her to complete the form and return it to him.

Questions to Consider

- How should the circulation clerk have handled this customer?
- Does the library have a policy concerning age qualifications for checking out a video?
- How do principles of intellectual freedom apply in this situation?
- How important is privacy in an interaction of this type?

Is there a better way to handle this situation? You decide.

9. Barker, *Paradigm Pioneers.*

10. Barker, *Discovering the Future.*

11. Barker, *Paradigm Pioneers.*

12. Barker, *Paradigm Pioneers.*

13. Barbara Conroy and Barbara Schindler Jones, *Improving Communication in the Library* (Phoenix: Oryx, 1986), 93.

14. Alvin Toffler, *The Adaptive Corporation* (New York: Bantam, 1985), 3.

15. Peter B. Vaill, *Managing as a Performing Art: New Ideas for a World of Chaotic Change* (San Francisco: Jossey-Bass, 1991), 55.

16. Sheldon A. Davis, "An Organic Problem-Solving Method of Organizational Change," in Warren G. Bennis and others, *The Planning of Change,* 2d ed. (New York: Holt, 1969), 358.

17. James C. Hansen and others, *Counseling: Theory and Process,* 2d ed. (Boston: Allyn and Bacon, 1977), 269–70.

18. Warren G. Bennis and others, *The Planning of Change,* 2d ed. (New York: Holt, 1969), 316.

6

⚹⚹⚹

Communication—
The Language of
Customer Service

Good customer service wears many faces: friendly staff, accurate information, convenient service, speedy response, and so forth. It is seen in both likely and unlikely places: a welcoming smile, a faxed magazine article, an adequate parking lot, a dial-in online public access catalog, and a bright and colorful interior—to name but a few. Empathy is essential to a successful response to customer needs and wants. Putting oneself in the place of the customer can work wonders for customer service, but for some staff members, it may not be easy to do.

Communication is the heart of customer service. This chapter will explore some of the ramifications of the "language" of customer service: communication that occurs through speech, body stance and motion, and active listening.

The Phases of Communication

Trying to discover customer needs, whether or not they have been expressed, leads directly into the communication area. It's widely understood that the only behavior that an individual can control is his or her own. Therefore, interacting with a customer requires that one's own negative or defensive emotions be held in check to respond positively to the customer's needs.

After the first contact with the customer, the second phase of communication occurs in what is traditionally called the "reference interview." This phase incorporates probing—focusing on the customer's specific wants or problems. By asking carefully formulated and open-ended questions—where the response requires more than a simple "yes"or "no"—it's possible to move beyond a single question and answer into a discussion. The examples in figure 6.1 illustrate the difference between closed and open-ended questions.

Figure 6.1   Closed and Open-Ended Questions

Closed Questions	*Open-Ended Questions*
Can I help you?	How can I help you today?
Is there a problem?	Would you please tell me about the problem that you have been experiencing?
Have you found what you are looking for in the computer catalog?	What have you found so far in the computer catalog?
Does it meet your needs?	How well does it meet your needs, and what other directions would you like to try?

Within this second phase of communication lie two essential assumptions: (1) that the librarian is fully knowledgeable about the numerous levels and dimensions of the library's products and services and (2) that the librarian not only understands the benefits to the customer that each product provides but can express that understanding clearly and concisely. Given those assumptions, you can clearly communicate aspects of the product to the customer.

However, one of the most powerful skills that librarians can develop is the ability to communicate explicit information in the needed form, at the time that it is needed, and without information overload. A second equally important skill is the ability to obtain, as well as to transmit, accurate and timely messages.[1] While you may know a lot about the product being offered to the customer, it is a distinct challenge to communicate appropriate information at the appropriate time.

The power of communication can also be a part of continuous quality improvement: every day seeking to find a way to improve the product. Improvement makes competitive products obsolete. The library that is not continually improving is not a "pioneer" and is gradually outdistanced by its competitors. When a library staff seeks to operate as pioneers—at the cutting edge of change—there are five steps to take:

1. Start with an open mind. Get outside your departmental borders. See what others are doing. Locate paradigm shifters and make friends with them.

2. Understand that you must break your patterns of the past to achieve future success. New rules will probably be brought to you by someone outside your organization.

3. Develop new reading habits—beyond your current boundaries. Read to see what new ideas are out there.

4. Be ready for failure, but remember that the gains will outweigh the losses in the long run.

5. Listen, listen, listen—to coworkers, customers, suppliers, and all external and internal customers.[2]

The pioneer role embraces what is possible, accepting whatever risks are involved. Mistakes will be made; judgments will be in error. But over the long term, "pushing the envelope" (to quote a trendy phrase today) is exciting and invigorating. The benefits you gain from being considered not only up-to-date but also a trendsetter will far outweigh those decisions that turned out to be not quite on target. The pioneering professional is energetic and enthusiastic about serving customers and sends very positive messages about the importance of the library in the community. Listening carefully to what both external and internal customers are saying is a first step into the dynamic and uncharted territory that beckons library pioneers.

Active Listening

Everyone listens—or thinks they do. Research shows that most people listen at 25 percent efficiency. This doesn't mean that they actually heard 25 percent of what was said but rather that of all they heard, they got 25 percent of it right.[3] The reality is that almost everyone physically hears; listening requires an additional ingredient: the act of attending. *Attending* means "paying attention, concentrating, focusing on what a person is saying." Most of us try to listen, but too often we are actually *planning* what we will say next. The result is that only part of the other person's message is getting through to us because a very real part of our consciousness is directed inward to our potential response.

Listening is even more difficult when our emotions or egos are involved. In this situation, the tendency to plan a rebuttal is still more pronounced. It is important to listen carefully, resisting distractions. Moreover, we must try to separate *what* is being said from *how* it is being said—i.e., the verbal message from the nonverbal message. Messages are being sent at both levels, and the careful listener can tune in to the complete message within the surrounding context.

Feedback is essential to active listening. To check on your perceptions, simple occasional questions, such as, "Do I understand that you are saying. . . ?" will help to clarify the communication exchange. If the other person affirms that your understanding is correct, active listening has taken place. However, if the other person says, "No, I didn't say that," the door is open for a dialogue that will better define and refine what is being said and improve mutual understanding.

Another helpful practice involves using the eyes rather than the mouth and vocal cords. Looking carefully at the person with whom you are communicating is essential to good communication and helps to read that person's nonverbal behavior. Not only can you discern subtle messages that are being sent but you can also begin to assess the other person's reactions to your comments. (A caveat: There are some cultures in which eye contact is considered to be impolite—or worse. Cultural sensitivity is essential to all types of communication; learning appropriate ways to connect verbally and nonverbally with another person is essential to good communication.) If it appears that your message is not getting across, try restating or paraphrasing it until an exchange of feedback makes it clear that messages are flowing back and forth in a climate of understanding.

The following suggestions can help improve listening skills.

Practice listening whenever you have the opportunity. As you listen, look for at least one good idea that you can use.

Give and ask for feedback as a part of listening. A request for feedback does not insult the speaker's intelligence; rather, it assures the speaker that you want to make certain that you have listened well and understand the intended meaning.

Try to listen from the speaker's frame of reference. Be continually on the alert to pick up all of the signals, listening for what is not said as well as for what is said.

Listen for concepts and main ideas rather than for facts and figures.

Listen fully and fairly to the message, and try not to be influenced by the package it comes in—i.e., poor grammar, an unpleasant voice, or the status level and credibility of the speaker.

Listen actively by asking clarifying questions and offering feedback. Understand the nature of the problem fully before offering advice.[4]

Listening is both an art and a skill. With practice, anyone can learn to be a good listener. It takes both a will and real commitment to make it happen, however. Librarians must ensure that they support staff in this endeavor—both by words and examples. Figure 6.2 provides examples of active listening.

Figure 6.2   Active Listening Responses

Problem

Rude patrons who don't want to wait their turn. They get impatient and it shows.

Implied criticism:	You must be incompetent or you wouldn't be so slow.
Patron's primary feeling:	Frustration, anxiety
Typical staff response:	Looks at patron who is in line and says "I'll be right with you," then when patron's turn comes (if he is still there) says, "May I help you?" (This is said coolly: response ignores the feeling.)
Active listening response:	Looks at patron who is in line and says, "I'll be right with you," then when patron's turn comes says, "I could see you were having a hard time waiting for me to get to you. Waiting in lines can be really frustrating. Now what can I do to help you?"

Problem

Patron wants you to find the information for him or her, particularly on the computer.

Implied criticism:	You should show more concern: you're inconsiderate and unfeeling.
Patron's primary feeling:	Scared, frustrated, anxious, bewildered.
Typical response:	"Try this and then let me know if you still need help."
Active listening response:	"I know that computers really frustrate some people. Let me repeat the steps for you one more time, then I need to get back to the desk. If you need more help later, let me know."

Problem

Phone caller wants you to leave the desk and get the information for him.

Implied criticism:	I am a taxpayer, and you should help me just as much as someone who is in the library. Why are you so inconsiderate? Lazy?
Patron's primary feeling:	Frustrated, inconvenienced
Typical response:	"We simply don't have enough people to give in-depth phone service. If you'll come to the library, we'll be glad to help you."

Active listening response:	"I know it must be frustrating to you and seem like an inconvenience to have to come down to the library for the information you need, but we simply don't have enough people to give in-depth phone service. If you'll come to the library, we'll be glad to help you."

Problem

Patron gets upset when you must refer him to another reference desk.

Implied criticism:	You are just like all the rest of the bureaucrats: you don't know anything, so we get the run-around.
Patron's primary feeling:	Frustrated, worried, concerned
Typical response:	"The information you need is found only in the government documents section."
Active listening response:	"Sounds as if you are worried about getting the runaround again. Let me call the government documents section to let them know you are coming."

Problem

Patron blames the reference librarian when it takes cataloging a long time to release a document.

Implied criticism:	If it is in the library, it should be available for checking out.
Patron's primary feeling:	Disappointed, frustrated
Typical response:	"It's not our fault. We can't do anything until cataloging releases it," or "It takes time to catalog—perhaps there is something else that will work for you."
Active listening response:	"I know it is frustrating. It frustrates me too because I like to give patrons what they need."

Problem

Patron brings incomplete information to library from her teacher and refuses to believe the teacher could be wrong.

Implied criticism:	If you were a competent librarian, I could get the information I need.
Patron's primary feeling:	Frustrated
Typical response:	"Are you sure you copied it right?"

continued

Figure 6.2 *continued*

Active listening response:	"I'll bet you are feeling very frustrated; I know I am. Let's call your instructor and verify the reference."

Problem

Patron is upset because the article he found in the index is one the library doesn't have, and it will take three or four weeks to get it through interlibrary loan.

Implied criticism:	Why don't you have what is in the indexes? It is not fair of you to get our hopes up and then let us down. You must not be a very good librarian.
Patron's primary feeling:	Frustrated, disappointed, anxious
Typical response:	"This is a national index, not one we produce locally; therefore, it indexes some journals that our library does not have. I can check to see if the University of Utah has what you want."
Active listening response:	"Sounds as if you are pretty disappointed. This situation comes up often and it always frustrates and challenges me. This is a national index, not one we produce locally; therefore, it indexes some journals that our library does not have. I can check to see if another university has what you want on interlibrary loan."

SOURCE: Nathan Smith, "Active Listening: Alleviating Patron Problems through Communication," in *Patron Behavior in Libraries: A Handbook of Positive Approaches to Negative Situations,* eds. Beth McNeil and Denise J. Johnson (Chicago: ALA, 1996), 131–3.

Nonverbal Communication Messages

Staff members not only must listen but need to *show* that they are listening. Good eye contact and appropriate encouraging responses are essential nonverbal communication strategies. Customers want to feel that they have the staff member's full attention and that they are important to the library staff.

Messages are continually being sent and received in libraries. In terms of customer service, these messages must be carefully crafted. The content of these interactions should be thought through (see "Ten 'Magic' Phrases" later in the chapter), but the "how" of the delivery can be just as important. Why is nonverbal communication so important? Consider the following:

70 to 93 percent or more of all communication is nonverbal.

We often make powerful, instantaneous, subconscious judgments about people based on their nonverbal communication.

Nonverbal behavior differs by culture.

The more diverse our customer base, the more likely we are to come into contact with nonverbal behavior unlike our own.

Interpreting nonverbal behavior of one culture to mean the same as that expressed by another culture is likely to be in error.[5]

Nonverbal responses may be intentional or unconscious, learned by imitation or done by accident. Such messages are received through all our senses, as illustrated by the following:

We see facial expressions, hand gestures, eye movements, and clothing.

We hear rate of speech and voice tone and pitch.

We may touch with a handshake or a hug.

We may smell perfume or lotion.[6]

The challenge we face is to correctly interpret these nonverbal messages. When we know someone well, we eventually develop— over time—a "dictionary" of meanings. But when we meet someone for the first time, our assumptions kick in, and we may easily misconstrue the meaning. For example, many of us sit with our arms crossed or folded. Are we hostile? bored? cold? unsure of what to do with our hands? Any of these possibilities could be in play. Therefore, we must resist making rapid assumptions and must investigate what is really going on. Particularly in situations where two or more cultural backgrounds are involved, nonverbal messages may be easily misdirected and misinterpreted. Caution and clarification are important attributes of an effective communication exchange.

Nonverbal messages can also be found in the library's setting. Is the exterior of the library clearly marked, neat, and inviting? Is the interior well-lighted, easy to navigate, colorful, and clean with good use of space and other design elements? When a customer walks in the door, will she or he experience feelings of welcome, friendliness, warmth? All nonverbal cues are not between people. A building (or an OPAC) sends numerous messages to the customer. Are we aware of what those messages are saying?

Feedback

"Are we aware . . ." can be asked of any communication exchange. How can we determine if the message (verbal or nonverbal) that we are sending has been accurately received? How can we be confident that we are understanding what the other person means? If we think of communication as a circle, rather than a straight line, this process becomes more understandable. Figure 6.3 illustrates the concept of the communication loop. The sender originates a message and selects a channel through which the message will be sent. This channel can be verbal, nonverbal, or mediated. However, a certain amount of interference is present in both the sender and the receiver. Perhaps either the sender or the receiver has a worry or a headache or has had an argument with a friend, a bout of the flu, a concern about a child . . . all of these and many more possibilities can interfere with the accuracy of either the sending action

Figure 6.3   The Communication Loop

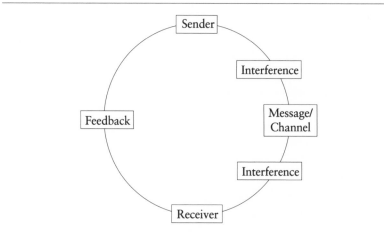

or the reception. The only way that the sender can be certain that the message is clearly received or that the receiver can be sure he or she understands the message is through the looping back function of feedback. Feedback checks on the message: how it is transmitted, how it is understood. If an irregularity or misunderstanding is discovered, the message can be re-sent, repeatedly if necessary, until both parties are comfortable with the communication.

Feedback is needed in every communication process, including that between library staff and customers. Continuous improvement is difficult to achieve without feedback; how else can the library staff know whether customers are satisfied? Staff, too, need to know whether they are individually making progress toward quality improvement and meeting the needs of customers. Feedback is an essential ingredient so that all parties are "on board" the *Quality Express!*

An Intercultural Challenge

Communicating across cultures may, at times, seem more than a challenge. It can be a frustrating experience for both parties as good intentions somehow become tangled and twisted, resulting in mixed signals and possible misinterpretations. When serving multicultural customers, some of the differences between cultures that need to be considered include

customer expectations based on cultural differences

individual and family values

language

protocol and courtesy

religious needs

communication style: verbal and nonverbal

logistical needs: currency, transportation, measurement systems, sizing

customs: food, holidays, rituals, and celebrations[7]

As an example, Scenario 6 illustrates how simple actions can be viewed very differently through dissimilar cultural eyes.

SCENARIO 6	
Two Viewpoints	
What Is Happening	*How It Is Interpreted*
Robert is a new circulation clerk at a branch of the municipal public library that serves new immigrants. A family that recently arrived from the Middle East enters the library. Robert smiles at the father, mother, and two little girls. The father asks where the travel books are located. Robert picks up some information on the library with his left hand and, with his index finger, beckons the family to follow him to the travel section. Robert is visibly shaken the next day when the library director takes him into the office and explains that a complaint has been lodged by the father, charging rude behavior and an insolent attitude.	Robert believes that he was friendly and welcoming to the new family. What he doesn't realize is that some of his behavior and gestures are considered impolite and inappropriate in the culture of the Middle East. Robert's smiling and open attitude toward the female members of the family was viewed as beyond the rules of propriety. When Robert picked up information brochures with his left hand, he was unaware that the left hand is reserved for personal hygiene in the country from which this family had journeyed. Finally, beckoning with an index finger is considered a degrading gesture.
Intended Result friendliness, helpfulness	*Interpretation* Insult and rudeness

It is important to remember that cultural differences may be present even between cultures that appear on the surface to be alike, such as between Anglo-Americans and Canadians. Sensitivity to differences among peoples is essential in a world that is rapidly becoming a large neighborhood due to telecommunications and vastly improved transportation systems. When it took hours, days, months, and even years to travel to a "foreign" location, there was time for the mind to adjust to new and unfamiliar circumstances. Today, however, in the blink of an eye—or a computer terminal—we encounter diverse peoples and expectations without time for psychological preparations. We must learn not only to cope with changing technology but also with interpersonal differences that are quite apart from our previous experiences.

How does culture influence us? Figure 6.4 presents ways in which the culture into which we are born influences how we think and behave.

With all these possible avenues for misinterpretation, how can we begin to learn new manners and ways of behaving? Following are some basic techniques to build upon in the learning process:

> Find out your customer's preferred way of being addressed and use it. How can you find this out? *Ask.*
>
> Pronounce names and titles correctly. Ask for feedback on how well you are (or are not) doing—and practice, practice, practice.
>
> Err on the side of formality. This may be difficult if your natural inclination is to be informal, but don't cross that line until your customer gives you permission.
>
> Avoid assuming. "Do unto others . . ." does not apply here. Your preferences are not necessarily the same as your customer's.
>
> Remember that "different" does not mean less valuable. Seek to understand, not to dismiss.
>
> Identify the assumptions that you personally hold about people. (See figure 6.4.) Check to see if they are true for each individual. (This is empathy.)[8]

Effective communication across cultures requires sensitivity, commitment, and a willingness to learn. But even within the same culture, multiple messages are sent—only a portion of which are verbal.

Ten "Magic" Phrases

Once the *process* of communication is comfortable for you— through lots and lots of practice—you can consider the content

Figure 6.4. How Culture Influences Us

Etiquette/Behavior	Beliefs/Values	Time	Communication	Human Relations
Greetings	What is beautiful	How scheduled	Language	Role of individual
Common courtesy	What is ugly	Importance	What said, unsaid	Roles of men
What is polite	Worthwhile goals	Tradition	"Small talk"	Behavior of men
Showing respect	Nature of Higher Being	Preparation	Direct or indirect	Roles of women
Embarrassment	(or religious figure)	for future	Formal vs. informal	Behavior of women
What/how we eat	Control vs. fate	Value of old age	Hand gestures	Harmony
Feeling good	Common sense		Facial expressions	Competition
Shopping/buying	Perceived needs		Nonverbal	Social class
Touching	Privacy		Frequency of smiles	Business hierarchy
Personal space	Health care		Recipients of smiles	Interaction with strangers
Posture	Personal hygiene		Meaning of smiles	Interaction with authority
Dress				Interaction with service
Holidays				persons
Celebrations				Relationships with friends
Use of money				Obligations to friends
Use of credit				Relationships with family
Use of bartering				Obligations to family
What is risqué				Crowd behavior
Use of health services				Audience behavior
Humor				
Use of mass transit				
Seating placement				

SOURCE: Leslie Aguilar and Linda Stokes, *Multicultural Customer Service: Providing Outstanding Service across Cultures* (Burr Ridge, Ill.: Irwin, 1996), 25–6.

of the message. Whether "magic" or not, there are certain phrases that have demonstrated their usefulness over the years. Some of these phrases are questions; others are simple statements. But in all cases, they focus on the customer and on continuous improvement of service. These are the ten "magic" phrases of customer service in the library.

1. *"Of course we can try to get it for you."*

   A sentence that should *never* be heard in a library without this corresponding phrase is "No, we don't have it." In other words, no customer should ever be turned away without the assurance that every effort will be made to satisfy his or her request.

2. *"How may I help you?"*

   This open-ended question is far superior to the commonly used, "May I help you?" The simple addition of "How" encourages dialogue and further discussion.

3. *"Of course we'll waive the fines . . . and I hope you are feeling better."*

   Every library should have a policy on fines and fees, even if none are to be assessed. Even when a well-written policy is in place, too many staff members interpret it literally and rigidly. Part of the language of the policy—supported by appropriate training and administrative support—should authorize staff to extend every courtesy to customers with special needs. Policies are intended to be guidelines, not commandments that can never be broken.

4. *"I'll be happy to make that call to _____ for you."*

   This is simple advocacy. Advocacy in the library environment does not mean practicing law. Rather, it is going the extra mile to make sure that the customer is connected with the appropriate referral—and then checking back with both the referral site and the customer to make sure that the information need was satisfied.

5. *"Did you locate what you wanted? How well does the material meet your needs? Is there something else that I can find for you?"*

This is a combination of closed and open-ended questions that probes into whether the customer has sufficient and appropriate materials. Too many items can be just as much of a problem as too few. Also consider the relationship between reading, listening, and viewing level and customer's age and ability. These phrases are also appropriate when the customer is browsing and engaged in self-service.

6. *"Is this what you are looking for, or shall I investigate further?"*

    These phrases further expand the type of interchange in the previous question and can be used quite effectively together in some cases. The compound question assumes that a staff member has been assisting the customer.

7. *"There are several possible ways to address your question. . . . Can you give me a little more background?"*

    This question continues to probe in greater depth to target appropriate material or information. It can be used together with the previous questions, or stand alone as an opening question.

8. *"I'm with a customer at the moment. . . . May I call you back in just a few minutes?"*

    "First come, first served" is more than simply logical; it is also courteous and considerate—to the in-library customer and to the customer on the telephone. However, an additional step should be taken. As soon as the first customer is served, the telephone customer should be called back. These sentences underscore the importance of each customer—but the follow-up service must also take place.

9. *"Yes, that item is in, and I'll be happy to hold it for you for forty-eight hours."*

    This simple statement demonstrates that several actions are taking place: (1) the staff member has looked for an item and been successful, (2) the customer cannot come to the library immediately and has asked that the item be held, (3) you have made an effort to be responsive to the convenience needs of the customer by holding the item for two days, and (4) you have clearly stated the length of the hold so that the customer understands the time parameters.

10. *"Thank you for using the 'XYZ' library."*

A simple phrase, yet one that is too infrequently expressed. We want our customers to come back and use the library often. This phrase acknowledges that the customer has choices and demonstrates gratitude for the patronage. (Is there any airline that does not thank customers as the airplane lands? If it works in the air, it can work on the ground!)

These phrases, in and of themselves, cannot guarantee good customer service. They can, however, go a long way toward helping achieve that goal. They may seem like common sense approaches, or ordinary service, to some—but they do serve as a measuring stick against which library staff members can measure their daily practices.

In the next chapter, many of the ideas presented in the first six chapters are revisited and distilled into "Strategies for Success"— a digest of concepts and tips that can be applied to the continuous quality improvement in customer service.

■ 6 ■

The Challenge of Diversity

Mike is a children's librarian who enjoys putting together storyhours for preschool children. One sunny afternoon, he welcomed some new children into the story circle. These children belonged to an immigrant family who had just moved into the neighborhood.

During the story hour, Mike used his considerable acting ability to enliven the storytelling. At the end of the session, the parents came into the story room to claim their children. Mike welcomed the immigrant parents to the library while establishing direct eye contact with both mother and father.

As an American, Mike had learned that to appear sincere and interested, he should look directly into the eyes of the person to whom he was talking.

The next day, the father was in the library with a formal complaint to the library director.

What has happened here?

One Possible Response

The library director, being a skilled interviewer, carefully questioned the irate father. She eventually learned that in the father's country direct eye contact was considered to be an insult. She apologized to the customer and gently assured him that the children's librarian did not understand these cultural customs. She assured the father that his customs would be taken into consideration in the future.

Questions to Consider

- How can a library staff keep track of demographic changes in the community?
- What are some ways that staff could be made aware of cultural differences?
- How important is staff training?
- Is cultural sensitivity a topic of discussion in your library?

Is there a better way to handle this situation? You decide.

Notes

1. Barbara Conroy and Barbara Schindler Jones, *Improving Communication in the Library* (Phoenix: Oryx, 1986), 4.

2. Joel A. Barker, *Paradigm Pioneers,* Discovering the Future Series (Burnsville, Minn.: Charthouse, 1993), video.

3. Conroy and Jones, 114.

4. Conroy and Jones, 116–17.

5. Leslie Aguilar and Linda Stokes, *Multicultural Customer Service: Providing Outstanding Service across Cultures,* Business Skills Express Series (Burr Ridge, Ill.: Irwin, 1996), 77.

6. Conroy and Jones, 120.

7. Aguilar and Stokes, 15.

8. Aguilar and Stokes, 19–20+.

7

❧⟨⟩❧

Strategies for Success

> What happens if you don't respond to customer concerns? What happens if you do not provide quality products and services at affordable prices? The answer is simple. You die.
>
> —*Bechtell, xiv.*

This chapter adopts a Janus-like profile, looking backward at the thoughts and ideas presented in chapters 1 through 6 and forward to a brighter tomorrow in which these principles are fully integrated into normal library operations. Connecting these two directions are strategies that, when put into practice, can put a library well on the road to success.

STRATEGY 1

Focus on the Customer

The cardinal rule of customer service is to always, at all times, focus on the customer (chapter 2). As simple as this may sound, it is the foundation for every other aspect of service. Keep these questions continually in mind: What does the customer want?

What does the customer need? What would make life easier for the customer? (Remember that there are internal as well as external customers.)

There are six techniques to ensure this focus:

1. *Be aware that your customer needs your attention.*

    A simple "Good afternoon. How can I assist you?" acknowledges the customer's presence. Practice using the language of customer service. (Chapter 6)

2. *Listen to understand.*

    Pay attention to what the customer is saying, rather than formulating your own response. Assume that you know nothing about what the customer may want; suppress any assumptions that you may have concerning the customer. (Chapter 6)

3. *Ask questions to gain information.*

    Ask clarifying and open-ended questions. Try to phrase your questions with potential benefits to the customer in mind. (Chapter 6)

4. *Acknowledge when things go wrong.*

    Things do not go right all of the time. When the inevitable happens, be honest and forthright with the customer. Expand upon a simple apology and assure the customer that you will make every effort to correct the situation— then follow through. (Chapter 5)

5. *Appreciate the customer.*

    Always remember that it is the customer who keeps the library in business. Let each customer know how much his or her patronage is valued, and thank the customer for using the library. (Chapter 6)

6. *Serve all customers as they wish to be served.*

    Every customer has individual needs and a unique cultural and experiential background. Remind yourself that each customer brings a unique set of needs and expectations to the transaction, and *never* assume that one customer is just like another.[1] (Chapter 2)

STRATEGY 2

Enhance Administrative Supports, Education, and Training

Introduce library staff members to the principles of customer service, and emphasize the level of administrative commitment behind the effort. Realign existing departments, functions, or duties as seems appropriate to improve service. Establish a training program for all staff that will support the customer service effort. Remember that compensation and reward systems speak loudly about administrative commitment and may need to be readjusted.

The library's internal stakeholders—*the staff*—are key to effective strategy making and implementation. In their study of America's best-run companies, Peters and Waterman state that, "There is no such thing as a good structural answer apart from people considerations, and vice versa. . . . Our research told us that any intelligent approach to organizing had to encompass, and treat as interdependent, at least seven variables: structure, strategy, people, management style, systems and procedures, guiding concepts and shared values (i.e., culture), and the present and hoped-for corporate strengths or skills."[2] Clearly, this interdependence among people and processes is vital to fostering strengths and improving areas of limitation. (Chapter 4)

STRATEGY 3

Identify Strengths and Limitations

Be honest and candid in determining where the library excels and where problem areas exist. (Chapter 3) Building upon strengths is a natural first step. Admitting to limitations allows for problem solving to begin. (Chapter 5) Both strengths and limitations can be related to the levels of available resources as well as outright service deficiencies. The use of teams can bring the knowledge and experience of multiple minds to the problem-solving effort. (Chapter 4)

Rosabeth Moss Kanter, a professor of management who has written extensively on organizational change, has determined that there are seven organizational attributes that are necessary to encourage innovation in an organization:

Being receptive to new ideas

Providing faster approval, reducing red tape

Collaborating between departments

Giving abundant praise and recognition

Providing advance warning of changes and open circulation of information

Making extra resources available

Having an attitude that we're always learning[3]

A library's staff that takes the time to identify strengths and weaknesses is likely to have an organization that is concerned with continuous improvement. These seven attributes can be the foundation of a strategic plan that will help the library shape its own destiny. (Chapter 5)

STRATEGY 4

Set Achievable Goals and Objectives

Once the library's strengths and limitations have been recognized, develop a blueprint of organizational activities that will outline opportunities for improving service quality and customer satisfaction. You may need to revise the mission statement to reflect new service thrusts. Whatever goals and objectives are proposed should lead to the development of measurable standards to evaluate customer service. (See Strategy 6.) After studying the results, select from among achievable change tactics and allocate sufficient resources to ensure success.

When improved quality is a major organizational thrust, several sets of questions need to be asked:

What is quality? How will you define it in your library?

How do you achieve the level of quality that you seek?

What will this effort cost? What are the opportunity costs? What are the costs of not improving quality?

What is your competition doing? What standards of quality are these competitors using? How do your standards compare?

STRATEGY 5

Commitment: Recognize and Acknowledge the Role of Will and Effort

What types of commitment might be needed? Consider the following:

a revised staff-reward system

adequate resources

redefined marketing strategies

changed product delivery systems

changed organizational structure

customer-focused staff training program

Many more items might be added to this list. It is important that all staff members "buy into" the effort to focus on customer service, devoting both intention and energy to accomplishing that goal.

In her video, Kanter also suggests that there are seven "ingredients" that individuals and organizations can put into practice that will facilitate change:

1. *Tuning into the environment*

    "Environmental scanning" is a trendy term, but the implications of being alert and sensitive to changing conditions are enormous. The ability to interpret the present in terms of possible futures is an essential skill for becoming a successful change agent.

2. *Kaleidoscope thinking*

    Most innovation is not the invention of a completely new idea; rather, it is the recombination of existing ideas into a new pattern or configuration. This reinterpretation of "what is" into "what could be" is the trademark of the inventor, the visionary—and the successful librarian.

3. *Communicating a clear vision*

    While a library's mission describes what the library is doing today, a vision portrays where the library intends to be in the future. All staff need to share and be committed to a single vision if progress is to be made.

4. *Building coalitions*

   To better use existing resources—particularly in this era of accountability—partnerships and relationships are essential within and outside the library setting. There is added strength in combining resources and talents. All parties, however, must be able to perceive both equity and benefits in the partnership arrangement.

5. *Working through teams*

   Several minds focused on a problem produce more potential solutions than do the sum of each person's individual ideas. The process of brainstorming and sharing is powerful; shared energies can get the job done in a timely way.

6. *Persisting and persevering*

   "Everything is a failure in the middle." The key is to keep on, experimenting and improving along the way, until a successful result emerges.

7. *Making everyone a hero*

   This sounds simple, but is too often absent in the workplace. Good ideas and great service need to be applauded in public—proudly and often. Appreciating and rewarding staff is a pleasure—and a responsibility of the effective manager.[4]

STRATEGY 6

Keep a Scorecard: How to Tell if You're Winning

When assessing your knowledge of customer needs and expectations, you must measure—evaluate—both what customers want and how well those wants are being met. Figure 7.1 provides a "scorecard" for assessing progress. Establish standards (see Strategy 4) and measure results against those standards. Creating a functional unit responsible for monitoring efforts can underscore the seriousness of your overall commitment.

Figure 7.1   Scorecard for Assessing Progress

AREA OF FOCUS:

Talk about the vision	The difference we want to make is . . .
	For these reasons . . .
Explore alternatives and design your approach	The best way to do this would be . . .
	For these reasons . . .
Learn from what's happening	The way we'll check on progress is . . .
	We can correct for problems by . . .
Let people know what happened	The way we'll document the difference we've made is . . .
	We'll communicate the difference by . . .
Integrate results with ongoing services	We'll take what we learned and relate it to the library as a whole by . . .
	The best way to integrate learnings would be . . .
Think about how it all worked	Improvements to be made in performance . . .
	Improvements to be made in planning . . .

!

SOURCE: Douglas Zweizig, Debra Wilcox Johnson, Jane Robbins with Michele Besant, *The Tell It! Manual: The Complete Program for Evaluating Library Performance* (Chicago: ALA, 1996), 106.

There are five critical success issues that face library managers who want to improve quality:

1. How big an investment is the library prepared to make? The level of investment can range from a token effort to a major commitment of money, time, talent, and energy. The library's administration must decide—and commit to—the magnitude of the venture.

2. How does the library gain and sustain executive commitment? Administrative supports—both verbal assurances and availability of sufficient resources—are essential to achieving quality customer service. A high level of support from the director's office is absolutely vital. Traveling to another library with a reputation for effective customer service is a good first step. Further steps can include attending training sessions, sitting in on customer focus groups, conducting employee briefing sessions to share views, and engaging in a staff retreat to focus on customer service.

3. How does the director activate the library's middle managers and leverage the initiative through their own energy and commitment? It is imperative that department heads and supervisors "buy into" the customer service effort or little will happen. The energies and commitment of these managers are essential if customer service is to improve. Special training sessions can be useful, in which managers are helped to focus on defining their customers, their missions, and their service strategies in light of perceived benefits.

4. How does the library avoid employee cynicism and earn acceptance and credibility in the minds of those who have to make it all happen? Staff who serve on the "front lines" can make or break service quality. Staff need to be engaged in quality thinking at the outset and have the opportunity to contribute their ideas. If the library has a history of soliciting staff input and not following through, this negative experience must be frankly acknowledged so that a clean start can be made. Ownership of the process at *all levels of staff* is critical to improving customer service.

5. How does the library sustain the momentum of the quality initiative when things get difficult? The effort to improve customer service will not proceed smoothly at all times; there will be rough spots and possible reversals to overcome. Managers get busy and can be distracted by problems and crises; staff can become fatigued or

impatient with the rate of progress. Yet it is crucial that the library administration involve all staff throughout the process: sharing information, asking for their help, giving them more authority and responsibility, nurturing their creativity, and investing in necessary training.[5]

Ultimately, consideration of these issues—plus the points that follow—will result in a customer service "scorecard." The additional points include the momentum of change in customer service practice; the level of reinforcement of the quality effort; the impact of designated resources; and the ultimate impact upon the customers, both internal and external, together with their responses.

STRATEGY 7

Work on Continuous Improvement

"Total quality management," so popular in the management literature, can be reframed as "total quality service." In Scenario 7, the simple act of putting an item on reserve is portrayed in terms of standard customer expectations—together with possible minus and plus factors. The notion of continuous quality improvement is a perpetually moving target. Is there ever a time when service is absolutely perfect? The combination of awareness and intent is powerful; staff members who vigorously seek to improve the level of service quality are to be commended—and rewarded—as the library moves closer to continuous improvement as an organizational mandate.

STRATEGY 8

Recognize the Power of the Customer

The newest trend in customer service is a one-to-one customer orientation. Also defined as a paradigm shift, this is a movement away from mass marketing to the idea that individualized one-to-one customer marketing is the direction of the 1990's.[6] In an era in which ideas are the medium of exchange, this new approach is a fundamentally different mode of competition in

SCENARIO 7		
Putting an Item on Reserve		
Minus Factors	*Standard Expectations*	*Plus Factors*
Waiting in line (in person or on telephone)	An apology for any delay	Cheerful staff
Form to fill out	As brief as possible	Handled by staff
Wait until item comes in	Prompt notification	Notification by telephone or E-mail
Item arrives when customer not in town	Item sent back	Item held for customer's return
Item arrives too late	Disappointment	(Discussion: What could be done?)

SOURCE: Adapted from Karl Albrecht, *The Only Thing That Matters: Bringing the Power of the Customer into the Center of Your Business* (New York: Harper, 1992), 220.

which "share of customer" (selling as many products as possible to a single customer) is the measure rather than share of market (selling your product to as many customers as possible). The underlying philosophy highlights the importance of the customer's power, and each customer's repeat business is the goal. (Chapter 2)

In such a model, dialogue and feedback are essential components of a collaborative information exchange. Both product and service quality are core to the concept. Short-term high levels of usage are less important than long-term customer retention. Once a customer uses the library, the goal is to keep that customer satisfied and using the library throughout his or her lifetime. The library's specific products will come and go as technologies change; only the customer can be constant.

It's important, as well, to recognize that customers often have a role in helping to design and produce the service that they consume. If customers can be viewed as "partial employees," then library staff can begin to think differently about what customers can contribute to the service encounter. Customers bring expectations and needs and can become involved as designers of policies and procedures through the expression of their expectations.

Transforming the Vision

The eight previously described strategies are the tools that the library can use to flesh out its vision. Ultimately, the vision needs to achieve the form and substance of reality. Band, in his book *Creating Value for Customers,* suggests this in a four-step process that is amplified here with a series of questions:[7]

1. *Understand customer expectations.*

    What do your library's customers require? Are you measuring your customers' wants, needs, and expectations? If no, start now! If yes, how are you using the results?

2. *Define satisfaction standards.*

    What are the library's strengths and weaknesses? What activities could you implement to identify opportunities for improving the value of library services and customer satisfaction? Is the library's mission statement stated in terms that describe the library's value to the community? Are measurable standards defined that will lead to identifiable results? Have appropriate strategies for change been selected? Are necessary resources commited?

3. *Match delivery to intent.*

    Have library staff members been introduced to the customer service improvement program? Has a training program been established? Have existing library departments been changed or realigned to improve customer service? Have the library's products and services been changed to feature quality? Has a person or persons been assigned the responsibility for monitoring quality? Have changes in the compensation and reward systems been initiated? Have promotion and marketing strategies been redefined to feature customer service? Have product delivery systems been refined with customer service in mind?

4. *Preach what you practice.*

Are library staff members telling customers what they have a right to expect? Are customers being assured that the library understands their wants, needs, and expectations? Have standards been clearly expressed and customers invited to judge the library based on those standards?

In another approach, the Columbus Metropolitan Library in Ohio has developed a five-step in-service program designed to help develop customer service skills for library staff. This program, known as CLASS (*C*ustomers *L*eaving *A*ppreciative, *S*atisfied, and *S*old), explores first impressions, interpersonal relationships, and communication. In brief, the five modules include

1. *May I Help You:* A module focusing on first impressions. Aspects of approachability are discussed, including library appearance, facial expressions, attire, attitude, body language, tone of voice, and the words used in greeting customers. The "show must go on," and library staff are urged to "feel it or fake it."

2. *What I Heard You Say Is:* A module concerning communication. Topics include active listening; telephone skills; the power of the smile in the voice; and hearing, interpreting, evaluating, and responding to messages.

3. *Customer Service Begins in the Workroom:* A module directed to the library's internal customers, the staff. Staff are recognized as all being part of one team, with good communication and frequent recognition as essential components. The message is given that, "It takes less time to be nice."

4. *Take Time to Know Us:* In this module, people are first. Emphasis is placed on special-needs populations and sensitivity awareness. Targeted segments of the community include multicultural populations, people with learning disabilities, children, homeless individuals, and

new readers. The underlying message is to avoid stereo-typing individuals as members of a predetermined "group" with common characteristics.

5. *Meeting the Challenge:* The final module focuses on customers who exhibit behavior that challenges the staff member's "zone of comfort." Positive stress reducers are introduced, and each customer is viewed as an opportunity for the staff member to grow as a customer service provider.[8]

CLASS is a good example of how in-service training can help library staff improve customer service excellence. It is only one example, however, and many similar training opportunities are available in the marketplace. The central thrust can be applied to all such continuing education programs: customer service excellence is essential to quality library operations.

Each of these strategies and approaches works. The key to success is to adapt what has been suggested by others, what has worked for others, and apply the ideas to *your* library. There are two questions that can be used by individuals (independently) and by the staff as a whole to assess how well the effort to improve is proceeding.

How have you improved your library's customer service in the past year?

What could you have done to improve—but have not done (yet)?

The responses to these two questions can lead to personal enlightenment and a fruitful staff discussion. When the goal is customer service excellence, transforming the vision into daily practice is not only desirable but absolutely essential if your library is to survive—and thrive—into the next century. Customer service excellence positions the library as a major player in the information industry and as a personal benefit to present and potential customers. It is not "whether" or "why," but "how" and "when" that will help the staff move toward customer service excellence.

■ 7 ■

The Case of the Cynical City Council

The Alphaville Public Library has a history of budget disagreements with the city council. The latest word from the council president involves a 20 percent reduction in next year's budget. The library director has argued that the library needs additional funds to compete in the information marketplace. Even though he has made a spirited appeal, his argument is rejected by the council.

Fact 1. There is little contact between the library and the city council except at budget time.

Fact 2. No member of the city council has a library card.

Fact 3. The council representative on the library board rarely comes to meetings.

What can the library director do to improve this situation?

One Possible Response

The library director enrolls in a marketing seminar; several special librarians are also enrolled. In the seminar, he learns about "SDI" (selective dissemination of information), which some of the special librarians use regularly with great success. SDI involves creating a profile on targeted customers that covers both professional and personal interests—and getting relevant information to them without being asked. He decides to experiment with SDI and creates a profile for each member of the city council. Council members are pleased to receive such timely and appropriate information.

Questions to Consider

- How could the library director not only register council members for library cards but also encourage use of the library?

- What can he do about getting the council representative to attend library board meetings?

- What kinds of contact with the city council members can be introduced by the library in nonbudget times to develop a positive relationship?

- What can the library do to be regarded as essential to the city council?

Is there a better way to handle this situation? You decide.

Notes

1. Leslie Aguilar and Linda Stokes, *Multicultural Customer Service: Providing Outstanding Service across Cultures,* Business Skills Express Series (Burr Ridge, Ill.: Irwin, 1996), 9–11.

2. Thomas J. Peters and Robert H. Waterman Jr., *In Search of Excellence: Lessons from America's Best-Run Companies* (New York: Warner, 1982), 9.

3. Rosabeth Moss Kanter, *The Changemasters: Understanding the Theory* (Chicago: Encyclopaedia Britannica, 1987), video.

4. Kanter.

5. Karl Albrecht, *The Only Thing That Matters: Bringing the Power of the Customer into the Center of Your Business* (New York: Harper, 1992), 207–15.

6. Don Peppers and Martha Rogers, *The One to One Future: Building Relationships One Customer at a Time* (New York: Bantam Doubleday Dell, 1995), audiotape.

7. William A. Band, *Creating Value for Customers* (New York: Wiley, 1991), 208–11.

8. Presented in a session given at the Public Library Association conference in Portland, Oregon, Mar. 1996.

8

Looking to the Future
through the Lens of
Customer Service

It is the year 2010. The information revolution is in full swing. Paradigms have shifted and shifted again. The volatility of the library's various environments creates perpetual challenge and uncertainty. The convergence of global markets and economic competition results in major shifts in political and societal circles. New technological developments pile one upon another as vendors seek to outperform each other. One question comes immediately to mind: Is there a library?

So much has been written regarding the imminent demise of the library, because of the Internet, the World Wide Web, and all the permutations that succeed them, that this is a very real question. While one set of forecasters predicts that the library is no longer necessary in a virtual world, there is another group that staunchly maintains that it is hard or impossible to kill off institutions. The reality probably lies somewhere in between.

Some librarians have worked diligently to create their version of an electronic or virtual library; yet there are still other librarians who view the notion of a virtual library as a threat.

Most would admit that the digital library era has begun. Many forecasters agree that declining costs and increasing performance in information technologies will probably continue for at least the next ten years without slowing down. This rapid development will produce new systems, services, and products. Without a doubt, what constitutes a librarian, a library, or a library customer will undergo substantial change.[1] To flow effectively with change that is both rapid and pervasive, it is necessary to adopt a futurist perspective.

Taking a Futurist Perspective

A futurist perspective is a sensitivity to the variety of possibilities that can emerge in the future. Developing this perspective requires an open mind, a willingness to consider more than one way of thinking and behaving, the use of present known information to forecast a desired tomorrow, and the commitment to work toward a preferred future and against other variations. Brodzinski, in his discussion of futures research, identifies five principles of planning for the future—within the caveats that futures techniques are no better than the data they use and that the futurist perspective must not be constrained by institutional traditions, values, and taboos.[2] His five principles will serve as a framework in this chapter for looking at the future through the lens of library customer service. Each principle will be examined in the context of not only library survival but the positioning of the library as an essential component of tomorrow's— and each customer's—world.

PRINCIPLE 1

> The future is determined by a combination of factors, not the least of which is human choice. What we decide today will have a significant effect tomorrow.

Certainly it is true that multiple factors transform our todays into our tomorrows. But choice is definitely central to the process—choices that the library staff makes and the choices available to each customer. Therefore, the decisions that determine present levels of customer service will have far-reaching impacts upon the near and long-term future and will affect the choices that present and potential customers make.

What are your present policies concerning customer service? What choices are you making now that will either enrich or restrict future operations? The other side of that coin is, What choices *could* you be making that would lead to a more positive position in your community and heightened customer satisfaction? It is absolutely vital that serious recognition be given to outcomes and consequences of present action and inaction. Scenario 8 provides a "reality check."

SCENARIO 8

A Look at Reality

How a Staff Member Sees It	*How a Customer Sees It*
I really would rather not work weekends and evenings.	If the library is not open when I can use it, I'll find my information elsewhere.
I have so much work to do, and there never seems to be enough time in the day.	I rarely ask questions of the library staff because they always seem so busy.
Books are appropriate in the library's collection; videos are frivolous.	It would be nice if the library had videos; since they don't, I'll have to rent them at the video store.
It's budget time and the city council should give the library more money; after all, the library is a good thing.	I don't want my taxes to go up. The library isn't important in my life, so why should I have to pay more taxes?
I wish (the customer) wouldn't keep asking for things we don't have; it takes time to request materials from other libraries.	I really need these materials; if this library can't get them, I'll try another library or order them from the bookstore.
Why should we have a display of third grade drawings? That's not what the library is for.	If my child's drawing is displayed in the library, I'll stop in to see it. Otherwise, I visit the library rarely.

It is equally essential that library staff members have an on-going realization that each customer has a variety of avenues to select from to satisfy informational, educational, and recreational needs. While the library is available to its entire customer base (as is any business), the reality is that market share is not as important as *share of customer*. It is actually a natural strategy for the library to take this approach: to identify a single customer, address a larger number of this customer's needs—both current and future, and try to develop products that respond to those needs.[3] Of course, the library serves many customers, but it is the approach of one-to-one customer service that is different from the more abstract notion of market share (in library terms, market share would be percent of the community holding library cards).

However, *multiple* transactions from the same customer are conditional upon the customer's satisfaction with *each* interaction. Each customer must be satisfied with the service received. Every customer is free to choose to withhold patronage at any time. It is excellence in customer service—excellence that will retain present customers and attract nonusers—that will propel your library into its desired future.

PRINCIPLE 2

There are alternative futures. There is always a range of decision and planning choices. We must seek out and determine these choices and select the best possible alternative.

Simply put, the attributes of the future are not a given. While it is true that the future will come whether or not we proactively work toward positive choices, its configuration may be unwelcome. The library that allows itself to drift from day to day, month to month, and year to year is the library that is not involved in creating its future. Library staff who wring their hands about change and try to maintain the status quo are denying themselves the opportunity to design the library's tomorrows.

It is important to recognize that indecision is, in fact, a decision—a decision not to take action. The inability to act, for whatever reason, can result in a self-fulfilling prophecy of uncertainty, doubt, and fear. There is always a temptation to wait for "the definitive technology," or to see how the library in the next town likes its new online system, or to delay significant customer service improvement until the beginning of a new planning cycle. Such waiting games are hazardous. As the rate of change increases, refusing to act will place the library farther and farther behind.

It is good management practice to identify as many of the possible choices as a reasonable period of time allows, but the next step is to take action. Even if the decision turns out to be less desirable than was hoped, the world will not end. A better perspective is to view both the decision and the outcome as additional data that will make the next decision a better one.

PRINCIPLE 3

> We operate within an interdependent, interrelated system. Any major decision, development, or force that affects any part of the system is likely to affect the entire system. We must be aware of changes not only in our own areas but in other areas within the system.

The system of information transfer is becoming increasingly complex. At one point in history, libraries and publishers composed the total information industry. Today, however, the library is simply one of the many players in an industry that includes competitors such as database developers, online services, the Internet, media producers, private entrepreneurs . . . and the list goes on.

Customers do, indeed, have many choices before them. It logically follows that a customer will seek out the provider that offers the greatest convenience, accuracy, and speed—at the most reasonable cost. While the library has a definite advantage in terms of cost, customers are placing more and more emphasis on the other factors.

Many of the changes facing libraries are rooted in technology. While this rapid development can appear on some days to be too much to handle, technology can provide not only problems but solutions as well. The concept of "share of customer" can be helped along by various media. Individually addressable electronic technologies (e.g., the Internet and fax today; interactive video, personal telephones, and other combinations of communications and computing tomorrow) will make interaction with customers a reasonable one-on-one activity. The information storage and retrieval marvels of this century will be supplemented and interconnected with these individually addressable media; the one-on-one customer future is upon us. In terms of interrelated system components, tomorrow will be so much more than a simple extension of today.

PRINCIPLE 4

> Tomorrow's problems are developing today. Minor problems ignored today may have catastrophic consequences five years from now. Gradual changes or distinct trends and developments cannot be ignored. We cannot allow ourselves to become preoccupied with immediate concerns. The near future must be an integral part of current decision making.

The notion of "not seeing the forest for the trees" certainly applies here. In libraries, it is all too easy to become absorbed in daily tasks and problems. Yet, the futuristic perspective is essential to make those decisions today that will so profoundly affect how tomorrow will unfold. In addition, the simple focus on analysis of service has become much more complex. The transactional encounter is still important, but it is now part of a much larger whole.[4]

Increasingly, the quest for service quality starts not internally, with an assessment of the library's strengths and weaknesses, but externally, in a vigorous quest for detailed knowledge of the customers themselves. The key to customer satisfaction is testing whether the library can discover, understand, and meet the customer's definition of minimum acceptable competence.

People and technology must be seen and managed as variable resources in the context of cost and value—provided or withheld based on what the customer really wants and is willing or able to pay for. There is a relationship between the level of quality and a matching ability/willingness to pay.

How and where the customer chooses to do business with the library is at issue, particularly as new ways to do business (the "virtual library") emerge at the same time that traditional settings (physical buildings and collection size) face overcapacity.

If the goal is to build lasting relationships with customers, those relationships must evolve into two-way exchanges incorporating mutual value and commitment. While "the customer is always right" is a core maxim of customer service, the truth is that the customer may *not* always be right (even though we behave as though that were true). Therefore, there is an element of customer education in providing good customer service in which library staff teach customers *how* to be right and empower them so that they *are* right.

Ultimately, long-term service quality depends upon the harmony and cooperative ventures developed between the library and its customers/stakeholders—the design and management of systems focused on developing excellence in customer service.

PRINCIPLE 5

We should regularly develop possible responses to potential changes. We should monitor trends and developments and not hesitate to use the collective creativity and judgment of our staffs to develop forecasts, projections, and predictions.

A new information technology paradigm has emerged from the convergence of technologies and business interests related to computers, communications, content, and consumer electronics. This new paradigm recognizes the impact of shifts in technologies, organizations, and economic activity.[5] Competitive forces have increased markedly due to the reshaping of traditional markets locally, regionally, nationally, and internationally. The library cannot ignore this transformation. Current decisions must be debated and made within the recognition of paradigm change.

As the "virtual library" evolves as one model of library service, there is a corresponding "virtual customer" who also emerges. Access, training, and expectations need to be addressed from the viewpoints of the library and its customers. Mission, community analysis, goals, values, policies, services, and procedures must be reexamined in the context of the new paradigm. Both library and customers need to commit to continuing learning and creative responses to change. While the process is challenging, it is also exciting with great potential for enhanced customer service.

Achieving and Keeping the Customer Service Advantage

First, a customer service advantage needs to be achieved, and then it must be constantly maintained. This advantage is based on customer knowledge, points and times of access, the cost/value ratio, competence of staff and technology, and the involvement of customers in the decision-making process. Figure 8.1 illustrates the components of customer service excellence; yet, none of these components is static, and all are subject to the ebb and flow of change. Not explicitly pictured in the diagram, but implied in the connecting lines, are factors such as promptness, accuracy, competence, communication, reliability, and responsiveness. The strategies offered by this book can be helpful in planning to achieve and keep customer service excellence, but the campaign must be engaged locally.

Figure 8.1   Customer Service Excellence

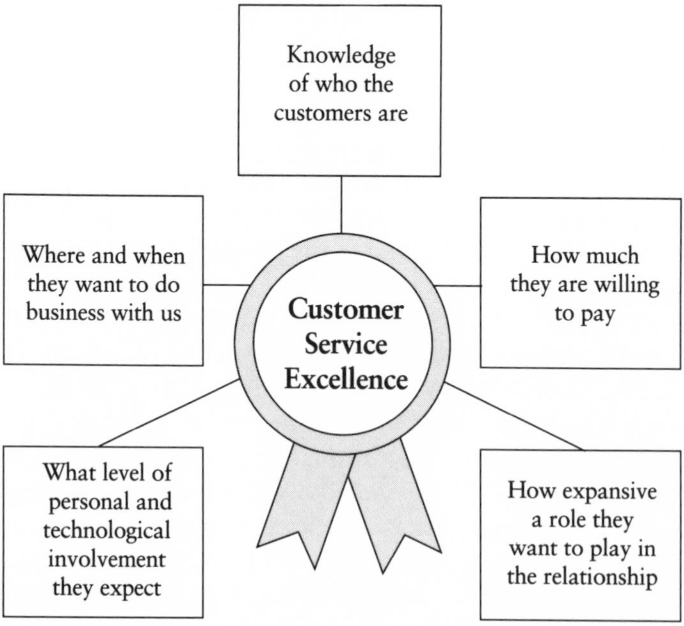

SOURCE: Adapted from Dick Schaaf, *Keeping the Edge: Giving Customers the Service They Demand* (New York: Dutton, 1995), 88.

However, the best intentions suffer from complacency if not given proper attention, and an advantage, once gained, can so easily slip away. Adopting a futurist perspective can go a long way toward keeping the customer service advantage and helping it grow. In the competitive marketplace, the advantage of customer service excellence is so precious that it can make the difference between surviving and thriving. Libraries that develop customers/stakeholders who are loyal and committed because of service excellence can move confidently into the new millennium.

It is a challenging time to manage libraries. To paraphrase Dickens, "It is the best of times, it is the worst of times." But libraries that have active partnerships with their customers can look forward to a hopeful future in which the dark corners are illuminated by the bright light of excellence.

▪ 8 ▪

A Study in Alternative Futures

The Greene Public Library is housed in a Carnegie-style building on Main Street. Services have been traditional: a collection composed mainly of books, programs centering on children, and special efforts for homebound and elderly citizens. The library is used primarily by citizens for recreational reading.

The city council has decided that all citizens should have Internet access. A citizens committee is being formed to look into the possibility of developing a freenet. The library staff is worried that this Internet project may take customers away from the library. However, they are also reluctant to become personally involved with the "Net."

What alternative futures exist for this library?

One Possible Response

The library director decides to request to be put on the citizens committee. The library staff feels relieved that this burden has been assumed by the director and "saved" them from some unnamed responsibility. They still worry that their work lives will somehow be affected by this technology.

Questions to Consider

- How relevant will the library appear to citizens' lives if the library is not actively involved in providing this service?
- How can the library staff be encouraged to embrace this change?
- What customers are likely to be attracted if the library provides Internet access?
- What are the political ramifications of action? Of inaction?
- Other considerations?

How should the library respond to this changing environment?
You decide.

Notes

1. Howard Harris, "Retraining Librarians to Meet the Needs of the Virtual Library Patron," *Information Technology and Libraries* 15, no. 1 (Mar. 1996): 48.

2. Frederick R. Brodzinski, "The Futurist Perspective and the Managerial Process," in *Utilizing Futures Research* (San Francisco: Jossey-Bass, 1979), 20–1.

3. Don Peppers and Martha Rogers, *The One to One Future: Building Relationships One Customer at a Time* (New York: Doubleday, 1993), 35–6.

4. Dick Schaaf, *Keeping the Edge: Giving Customers the Service They Demand* (New York: Dutton, 1995), 4–5, 23–4.

5. Harris, 49.

For Further Reading

Achieving Breakthrough Service in Libraries. Chicago: ALA, 1994. Video.

Aguilar, Leslie, and Linda Stokes. *Multicultural Customer Service: Providing Outstanding Service across Cultures*. Business Skills Express Series. Burr Ridge, Ill.: Irwin, 1996.

Albrecht, Karl. *At America's Service*. Homewood, Ill.: Dow Jones-Irwin, 1988.

————. *The Only Thing That Matters: Bringing the Power of the Customer into the Center of Your Business*. New York: Harper, 1992.

Albrecht, Karl, and Lawrence J. Bradford. *The Service Advantage: How to Identify and Fulfill Customer Needs*. Homewood, Ill.: Dow Jones-Irwin, 1990.

Albrecht, Karl, and Ron Zemke. *Service America! Doing Business in the New Economy*. Homewood, Ill.: Dow Jones-Irwin, 1985.

Albrecht, Steven. *Service, Service, Service: The Growing Business' Secret Weapon*. Holbrook, Mass.: Bob Adams, 1994.

Arogyaswamy, Bernard, and Ron P. Simmons. *Value-Directed Management: Organizations, Customers, and Quality*. Westport, Conn.: Quorum, 1993.

Band, William A. *Creating Value for Customers*. New York: Wiley, 1991.

————. *Touchstones: Ten New Ideas Revolutionizing Business.* New York: Wiley, 1994.

Barker, Joel A. *Discovering the Future: The Business of Paradigms.* 2d ed. Burnsville, Minn.: Infinity Ltd. and Charthouse, 1989. Video.

————. *Paradigm Pioneers.* Discovering the Future Series. Burnsville, Minn.: Charthouse, 1993.

Bechtell, Michele L. *Untangling Organizational Gridlock: Strategies for Building a Customer Focus.* Milwaukee, Wisc.: ASQC Quality Pr., 1993.

Bennis, Warren G., et al. *The Planning of Change.* 2d ed. New York: Holt, 1969.

Berry, Dick. *Managing Service for Results.* Research Triangle Park, N.C.: Instrument Society of America, 1983.

Bhote, Keki R. *Next Operation as Customer (NOAC): How to Improve Quality Cost and Cycle Time In Service Operations.* New York: American Management Association, 1991.

Blanchard, Ken, and Sheldon Bowles. *Raving Fans: A Revolutionary Approach to Customer Service.* New York: William Morrow, 1993.

Blanding, Warren. *Practical Handbook of Customer Service Operations: Translating Excellence into Action.* Washington, D.C.: International Thomson Transport Pr., 1989.

Bok, Derek. *The Cost of Talent.* New York: Free Press, 1993.

Brody, E. S. *Communication Tomorrow: New Audiences, New Technologies, New Media.* New York: Praeger, 1990.

Broydrick, Stephen C. *How May I Help You? Providing Personal Service in an Impersonal World.* New York: Irwin, 1994.

Brown, Tom J., Gilbert A. Churchill Jr., and J. Paul Peter. *Improving the Measurement of Service Quality.* Working Paper #92-4. Madison, Wisc.: The University of Wisconsin–Madison School of Business, 1992.

Buckland, Michael. *Redesigning Library Services: A Manifesto.* Chicago: ALA, 1992.

Cannie, Joan Koob, with Donald Caplin. *Keeping Customers for Life.* New York: American Management Assn., 1991.

Carlzon, Jan. *Moments of Truth.* Cambridge, Mass.: Ballinger, 1987.

Chin, Robert, and Kenneth D. Benne. "General Strategies for Effecting Changes in Human Systems." In Warren G. Bennis and others, *The Planning of Change.* 2d ed. New York: Holt, 1969.

Conroy, Barbara, and Barbara Schindler Jones. *Improving Communication in the Library.* Phoenix: Oryx, 1986.

Davidow, William H., and Bro Uttal. *Total Customer Service: The Ultimate Weapon.* New York: Harper, 1989.

Davis, Sheldon A. "An Organic Problem-Solving Method of Organizational Change." In Warren G. Bennis and others, *The Planning of Change.* 2d ed. New York: Holt, 1969.

Davis, Stanley M. *Future Perfect.* Reading, Mass.: Addison-Wesley, 1987.

Desatnick, Robert L., and Denis H. Detzel. *Managing to Keep the Customer: How to Achieve and Maintain Superior Customer Service throughout the Organization.* Rev. ed. San Francisco: Jossey-Bass, 1993.

Dobyns, Lloyd, and Clare Crawford-Mason. *Quality or Else.* Boston: Houghton Mifflin, 1991.

Dougherty, Richard M., and Fred J. Heinritz. "Scientific Management of Library Operations." In Beverly P. Lynch, *Management Strategies for Libraries.* New York: Neal-Schuman, 1985.

Eastman Kodak. *Keeping the Customer Satisfied—A Guide to Field Service.* Milwaukee, Wisc.: ASQC Quality Pr., 1989.

Erikson, Erik H. *Childhood and Society.* 2d ed. New York: Norton, 1963.

———. *Identity: Youth and Crisis.* New York: Norton, 1968.

Garvin, David. *Managing Quality: The Strategic and Competitive Edge.* New York: Free Press, 1988.

Gould, Roger. *Transformations: Growth and Change in Adult Life.* New York: Simon & Schuster, 1978.

Grönroos, Christian. *Service Management and Marketing: Managing the Moments of Truth in Service Competition.* Lexington, Mass.: Lexington Books, 1990.

Hammer, Michael, and James Champy. *Reengineering the Corporation.* New York: Harper, 1993.

Hansen, James C., and others. *Counseling: Theory and Process.* 2d ed. Boston: Allyn and Bacon, 1977.

Harris, Howard. "Retraining Librarians to Meet the Needs of the Virtual Library Patron," *Information Technology and Libraries.* 15, no. 1 (Mar. 1996).

Heskett, James L., W. Earl Sasser Jr., and Christopher W. L. Hart. *Service Breakthroughs: Changing the Rules of the Game.* New York: Free Press, 1990.

Kanter, Rosabeth Moss. *The Change Masters: Innovation for Productivity in the American Corporation.* New York: Simon & Schuster, 1983.

———. *The Changemasters: Understanding the Theory.* Chicago: Encyclopaedia Britannica, 1987. Video.

Kidd, J. R. *How Adults Learn.* New York: Association Pr., 1973.

Kohn, Alfie. *Punished by Rewards.* New York: Houghton Mifflin, 1993.

Kotler, Philip. *Marketing for Nonprofit Organizations.* 2d ed. Englewood Cliffs, N.J.: Prentice-Hall, 1982.

Kotler, Philip, and Alan R. Andreasen. *Strategic Marketing for Nonprofit Organizations.* 3d ed. Englewood Cliffs, N.J.: Prentice-Hall, 1987.

Kuhn, Thomas. *The Structure of Scientific Revolutions.* 2d ed. Chicago: Univ. of Chicago Pr., 1970.

Leppard, John, and Liz Molyneux. *Auditing Your Customer Service.* New York: Routledge, 1994.

Levinson, Daniel J., and others. *The Seasons of a Man's Life.* New York: Knopf, 1978.

Lovelock, Christopher H. *Services Marketing.* Englewood Cliffs, N.J.: Prentice-Hall, 1984.

MacNeill, Debra J. *Customer Service Excellence.* Burr Ridge, Ill.: Irwin, 1994.

McKenna, Regis. *Relationship Marketing: Successful Strategies for the Age of the Customer.* New York: Addison-Wesley, 1991.

Naisbett, John. *Megatrends: Ten New Directions Transforming Our Lives.* New York: Warner, 1982.

Neugarten, Bernice, ed. *Middle Age and Aging.* Chicago: Univ. of Chicago Pr., 1966.

Peppers, Don, and Martha Rogers. *The One to One Future: Building Relationships One Customer at a Time.* New York: Doubleday, 1993.

———. *The One to One Future: Building Relationships One Customer at a Time.* New York: Bantam Doubleday Dell, 1995. Audiotape.

Peters, Thomas J., and Robert H. Waterman Jr. *In Search of Excellence: Lessons from America's Best-Run Companies.* New York: Warner, 1982.

Rapp, Stan, and Tom Collins. *The Great Marketing Turnaround: The Age of the Individual and How to Profit from It.* Englewood Cliffs, N.J.: Prentice-Hall, 1990.

Ries, Al, and Jack Trout. *Bottom-Up Marketing.* New York: McGraw-Hill, 1989.

Robinson, Russell D. *An Introduction to Helping Adults Learn and Change.* Milwaukee, Wisc.: Omnibook, 1979.

Schaaf, Dick. *Keeping the Edge: Giving Customers the Service They Demand.* New York: Dutton, 1995.

Schneider, Benjamin, and David E. Bowen. *Winning the Service Game.* Boston: Harvard Bus. School Pr., 1995.

Schultz, Louis E. *Profiles in Quality: Learning from the Masters.* White Plains, N.Y.: Quality Resources, 1994.

Sewell, Carl, and Paul B. Brown. *Customers for Life: How to Turn That One-Time Buyer into a Lifetime Customer.* New York: Doubleday, 1990.

Sheehy, Gail. *New Passages: Mapping Your Life across Time.* New York: Random, 1995.

————. *Passages: Predictable Crises of Adult Life.* New York: Hart, 1972.

Sutton, Brett. *Public Library Planning: Case Studies for Management.* Westport, Conn.: Greenwood, 1995.

Toffler, Alvin. *The Adaptive Corporation.* New York: Bantam, 1985.

Trezza, Alphonse F., ed. *Commitment to Service: The Library's Mission.* Boston: G. K. Hall, 1990.

Vaill, Peter B. *Managing as a Performing Art: New Ideas for a World of Chaotic Change.* San Francisco: Jossey-Bass, 1991.

Vaillant, George E. *Adaptation to Life: How the Best and the Brightest Came of Age.* Boston: Little, Brown, 1977.

Vavra, Terry G. *Aftermarketing: How to Keep Customers for Life through Relationship Marketing.* Chicago: Business One/Irwin, 1992.

Weingand, Darlene E. *Marketing/Planning Library and Information Services.* Littleton, Colo.: Libraries Unltd., 1987.

Index

Note: Page references in *italics* indicate figures.

A

access paradigms, 69, 70
accuracy, 120
active listening, 82–6
    responses, *84–6*
adaptability (of contact
    personnel), 28
administrative support, 100, 105
    of teams, 53–5
advocacy, 93
aesthetic values, 21, 39–40
Albrecht, Karl, 3–4, 15
alternative futures, 116–17, *122*
ambiguity, 41
appreciation (of customers), 99
architecture (of library), 38–9
assumptions, 99
atmospherics, 38–40
attending, 82
attitudes (of employees), 4
augmented product, 36–8
automation. *See* technology
availability (of service), 26

B

Band, William A., 28–9, 33–4,
    108–9
Barker, Joel A., 69–71
beliefs (of employees), 4
Berry, Dick, 40
Brodzinski, Frederick R., 114–19
Buckland, Michael, 9, 23
budget (and product mix), 35–6

C

change, 7–10
    management of, 75
    organizational receptiveness to,
        100–1
    scenario, 10
choice, 114–17
CLASS (Customers Leaving
    Appreciative, Satisfied, and
    Sold), 109–10
closed questions, *80*
coalitions, 103
collection paradigms, 70

131

Columbus (Ohio) Metropolitan
    Library, 109
commitment (to customer service),
    102–3, 105
communication, 5, 75–6, 79–97,
    109, 120
    active listening, 82–6
    and contact personnel, 28
    and cultural differences, 82–3,
        87, 89–91, 92
    feedback, 5–6, 82–3, 88–9
    "magic" phrases, 91–5
    nonverbal, 86–8
    phases of, 79–81
communication loop, *88*
competence, 120
competition
    for customers, 32, 101
    among staff, 45–6
concepts (guiding), 48, 100
conflict (management of), 71–5
    within teams, 57
confrontation, 74–5
congruence, 41
contact personnel, 27–8
    See also staff
continuous improvement, 58, 101,
    106
control (of staff), 7
cooperation (among staff), 46
core product, 36–7
"Cosmology and the Changing
    Role of Libraries," 7–8
costs (of quality), 101
courtesy, 26
Creating Value for Customers,
    28–9, 33–4, 108–9
culture, 92
    and communication, 82–3, 87,
        89–91
    differences in, 19–20
    of organization, 4, 5–7, 100
customer (as a word), 2
customer frustration list, 73
"customer is always right," 26–8,
    119
customer needs, 8, 32

customer satisfaction, 26, 32,
    40–1, 118
    measuring, 28–9
customer service
    and contact personnel, 27
    in electronic age, 24–5
    equation, 8, 32
    improvements in, 58
    integration into library
        operations, 55–7
    philosophy of, 1–11
customer service advantage,
    120–1
customers
    appreciation of, 99
    and changing environment,
        23–6
    expectations of, 28, 108
    external, 14
    focus on, 13–31, 98–9
    hierarchy of values, 15
    identification of, 14
    internal, 14, 109
    knowledge of, 22, 120
    perceptions of, 28
    power of, 106–8
    work habits of, 24

D
data
    analysis of, 67
    collection of, 65–6, 67
    interpretation of, 68
    and paradigms, 68–70
Davis, Sheldon A., 73
defensiveness, 74
deliverable values, 21
diversity (of customers), 19–20,
    109
Dooley, J. F., 7–8
durability, 26
Dynamic System Theory, 5

E
ease of repair, 26
ease of use, 26

education, 100
    See also training
electronic age
    customer service in, 24–5
    See also future
emotions (and conflict), 73–5
empathy, 79, 91
employees. *See* staff
empowerment (staff), 5, 6, 7, 93
environment
    awareness of, 102
    changing, 7–10, 23–6, 32
    customers in, 23–6
    library, 38–40
environmental scanning, 102
environmental values, 21
Erikson, Erik H., 17
ethnicity (differences in), 19–20
evaluation (of customer service
    quality), 103
excellence (customer service), 8, 9,
    32–43, 110, *120*
expectations (customer) 108
    changing nature of, 25, 41
experiences (life), 20–1
external customers, 14

F
feedback, 5–6, 82–3, 88–9
    See also communication
feeling (of library), 39
financial values, 21
first impressions, 109
flow (of library), 39
focus (on customer), 98–9
focus groups, 16
Franklin, Hardy, 2–3
frustration (of customers), *73*
functionality (of library), 39
future, 113–23
    alternative, 116–17, *122*
futurist perspective, 114–19, 121

G
Gerhardt, Lillian N., 2–3
goals, 101

Gould, Roger, 17
guiding concepts, 48, 100

H
hierarchy of customer values, *15*
hierarchy of human needs, 15, 16,
    17
human development, 16–19

I
improvements (in customer
    service), *58*
    See also continuous
        improvement
information (among staff), 47
informational values, 21
innovation, 102
input, 6
    in communication, 5
intangible products, 36–8
intensity, 41
interdependence, 46
internal customers, 14, 109
interpersonal relationships, 109
interpersonal values, 21
interpretation (of research results),
    68
*An Introduction to Helping
    Adults Learn and Change,* 17
investment (in customer service),
    104

K
Kanter, Rosabeth Moss, 100–1,
    102–3
knowledge (staff), 47
Kotler, Philip, 34–5, 38

L
language (of customer service),
    2–3
leadership, 7, 72
Levinson, Daniel J., 17
libraries
    competition of, 3
    future of, 113

life
    experiences, 20–1
    stages in, 18–19
limitations (organizational),
    100–1, 108
listening (active), 82–6, 99
    responses, *84–6*
Lucier, R. E., 7, 8

M
"magic" phrases, 91–5
management, 7, 72
management style, 48, 51–2, 100
Managing Service for Results, 40
*Marketing for Nonprofit
    Organizations*, 34–5
Maslow, Abraham, 15, 16
matrix model, 49, *50*
measurement (of customer service
    quality), 103
mission, 21–3, 101
    paradigms, 70
morale (staff), 5
Myers-Briggs (MBTI) instrument,
    51

N
Neugarten, Bernice, 17
*New Passages: Mapping Your Life
    Across Time*, 17
nominal group technique, 53
nonverbal communication, 86–8

O
objectives, 101
*The Only Thing That Matters:
    Bringing the Power of the
    Customer into the Center of
    Your Business*, 3–4, 15
open-ended questions, *80*, 99
orbit model, 49
ownership (staff), 105

P
paradigm
    pioneers, 71
    shifts, 69–70, *70*

paradigms, 68–71
    access, 70
    collection, 70
    and data, 68, 70
    language, 3
    mission, 70
    staffing, 70
    and technology, 119
*Passages: Predictable Crises of
    Adult Life*, 17
patron (as a word), 2, 14
people, 48, 51, 100
performance, 26
periodicity, 41
permission (in training teams), 57
perseverance, 103
Peters, Thomas J., 48, 100
philosophy (of customer service),
    1–11
pioneers
    individuals as, 71
    libraries as, 81
planning, 9, 63–4
    and mission, 21–3
    teams, 14–15
point of view, 74, 115
power
    of customer, 106–7
    of staff, 47
problems (of the future), 118
problem solving, 62–78
procedural values, 21
procedures, 48, 52–3, 100
product item, 35
product line, 35
product mix, 3, 35
products (library), 34–8
promptness, 26, 120
prosperity, 8–9, 32
Public Library Planning, 63–4

Q
quality (of service), 25, 32, 33–4,
    101
    costs of, 101
questionnaire (customer service),
    67

questions
    closed, *80*
    open-ended, *80, 99*

R
Rauscher, Robert J., *5*
reality, *5, 6, 7*
receptiveness to change
    (organizational), 100–1
recognition (of staff), 103
reference interview, 80
reliability, 120
research
    exploratory, 66–7
    framework, 65–8
    instrument (design of), 67
    objectives, 65
    and problem solving, 64–8
responsiveness, 120
rewards (staff), 47
Robinson, Russell, 16–17

S
scorecard, 103–6, *104*
In Search of Excellence, 48
secondary data search, 65–6
selective dissemination of
    information (SDI), 22
sensitivity (of contact personnel),
    28
service
    definitions of, 1
    strategy, 23
    trouble-free, 26
setting (library), 87–8
share of customers, 116, 117
Sheehy, Gail, 17–19
smile, 40–1
space (library), 38–40
spirit (of service), 4
spiritual continuum, *4*
staff, 100, 109, 110
    behavior of, 45–6
    contact personnel, 27–8
    empowerment of, 5, 6, 7, 93
    involvement of, 47
    relationships with customers, 57

and spirit of service, 4
staffing paradigms, 70
stages (life), 18–19
stakeholders, 56, 57–9
standards, 108
strategic plan. *See* planning
strategies (for success), 48,
    98–112
    in team building, 50–1
strengths (of organization), 52,
    100–1, 108
structure (organizational), 48–50,
    100
success
    issues, 104–6
    strategies for, 98–112
survival, 8–9, 32
Sutton, Brett, 63–4
systems, 48, 52–3, 100

T
tangible product, 36–8
target groups, 67
teams, 44–61, 100, 103
    and administrative support,
        53–5
    charge of, 52
    climate of, 53
    composition of, 52
    expectations of, 52
    formation of, 47–53
    and management style, 51–2
    members of, 48, 51
    and nominal group technique,
        53
    and organizational structure,
        48–50
    planning, 14–15
    size of, 52
    strategy in building, 50–1
    support of, 52–3
technology, 9, 23–5, 117, 119
    and customer requirements, 25
TELL IT!, *104*
terminology (in libraries), 2
Toffler, Alvin, 72
training, 55, 57, 100

U
user (as a word), 2

V
Vaillant, George E., 17
values
    aesthetic, 21, 39–40
    customer, 15–16, 21
    deliverable, 21
    environmental, 21
    financial, 21
    informational, 21
    interpersonal, 21
    procedural, 21
    staff, 4, 48, 100
virtual customer, 119
virtual library, 113, 119
vision, 57, 102–3, 108–10

W
warranty, 26
Waterman, Robert H., Jr., 48, 100
weaknesses (organizational),
    100–1, 108

Darlene E. Weingand is professor at the University of Wisconsin–Madison School of Library and Information Studies (SLIS) and is the faculty director of SLIS Continuing Education Services. She teaches library management and marketing to librarians in all types of libraries and has written extensively in these areas. Other books include *Administration of the Small Public Library*, third edition (ALA, 1992); *Managing Today's Public Library: Blueprint for Change* (Libraries Unlimited, 1994); and *Literacy and Cultural Heritage* (Scarecrow Press, 1992). Weingand has earned national and international recognition for her work.